EXERCISES IN ENGLISH

LOYOLA PRESS.

Consultants
Therese Elizabeth Bauer
Martina Anne Erdlen
Anita Patrick Gallagher
Patricia Healey
Irene Kervick
Susan Platt

Linguistics Advisor
Timothy G. Collins
National-Louis University

Editors
Allison Kessel Clark
Beth Renaldi
Ron Watson

Series Design: Loyola Press
Interior Art: Jim Mitchell: 1, 5, 15, 29, 41, 77, 84, 91
All interior illustrations not listed above are ©iStockphoto.com

ISBN-13: 978-0-8294-3627-3; ISBN-10: 0-8294-3627-8

Manufactured in the United States of America.

LOYOLA PRESS.
3441 N. Ashland Avenue
Chicago, Illinois 60657
(800) 621-1008
www.loyolapress.com

12 13 14 15 16 17 RRD 10 9 8 7 6 5 4 3 2 1

Contents

SENTENCES

1 Sentences 1
2 Statements and Questions 2
3 Question Words 3
4 Commands 4
5 Exclamations 5
6 Kinds of Sentences 6
7 Subjects 7
8 Predicates 8
9 Combining Predicates 9
10 Combining Subjects 10
11 Combining Sentences 11
12 Avoiding Run-on Sentences 12
13 Reviewing Sentences 13

NOUNS

14 Nouns 15
15 Proper Nouns and Common Nouns 16
16 Singular Nouns and Plural Nouns 17
17 More Plural Nouns 18
18 Irregular Plural Nouns 19
19 Singular Possessive Nouns 20
20 Plural Possessive Nouns 21
21 Irregular Plural Possessive Nouns 22
22 Singular Possessive Nouns and Plural Possessive Nouns 23
23 Collective Nouns 24
24 Nouns as Subjects 25
25 Words Used as Nouns and Verbs 26
26 Reviewing Nouns 27

PRONOUNS

27 Singular Pronouns 29
28 Plural Pronouns 30
29 Subject Pronouns 31
30 Object Pronouns 32
31 Possessive Pronouns 33
32 Possessive Adjectives 34
33 Agreement of Pronouns and Verbs 35
34 *I* and *Me* 36
35 Compound Subjects 37
36 Compound Objects 38
37 Reviewing Pronouns 39

VERBS

38 Verbs 41
39 Action Verbs 42
40 More Action Verbs 43
41 Being Verbs 44
42 Helping Verbs 45
43 Principal Parts of Verbs 46
44 Regular and Irregular Verbs 47
45 *Bring* 48
46 *Buy* 49
47 *Come* 50
48 *Sit* 51
49 *Eat* 52
50 *Go* 53
51 *See* 54
52 *Take* 55
53 *Tear* 56

54 *Write* 57
55 Irregular Verbs 58
56 Simple Present Tense 59
57 Simple Past Tense 60
58 Future Tense with *Will* 61
59 Future Tense with *Going To* 62
60 Present Progressive Tense 63
61 Past Progressive Tense 64
62 *Is* and *Are, Was* and *Were* 65
63 Contractions with *Not* 66
64 Reviewing Verbs 67

ADJECTIVES

65 Adjectives 69
66 Adjectives Before Nouns 70
67 Subject Complements 71
68 Compound Subject Complements 72
69 Adjectives That Compare 73
70 More Adjectives That Compare 74
71 Irregular Adjectives That Compare 75
72 Adjectives That Tell How Many 76
73 Articles 77
74 Demonstrative Adjectives 78
75 Proper Adjectives 79
76 Nouns Used as Adjectives 80
77 Reviewing Adjectives 81

ADVERBS AND CONJUNCTIONS

78 Adverbs 83
79 Adverbs That Tell *When* or *How Often* 84
80 Adverbs That Tell *Where* 85
81 Adverbs That Tell *How* 86
82 More Adverbs 87
83 Negatives 88
84 *Good* and *Well* 89
85 *To, Too,* and *Two* 90
86 *Their* and *There* 91
87 Coordinating Conjunctions 92
88 Reviewing Adverbs 93

PUNCTUATION, CAPITALIZATION, ABBREVIATIONS

89 End Punctuation 95
90 Capital Letters—Part I 96
91 Capital Letters—Part II 97
92 Capital Letters—Part III 98
93 Abbreviations 99
94 More Abbreviations 100
95 Titles and Initials 101
96 Titles of Books and Poems 102
97 More Titles of Books and Poems 103
98 Commas in a Series 104
99 Commas in Direct Address 105
100 Commas in Compound Sentences 106
101 Apostrophes 107
102 Addresses 108
103 Direct Quotations 109
104 More Direct Quotations 110
105 Reviewing Punctuation, Capitalization, and Abbreviations 111

DIAGRAMMING

106 Subjects and Predicates 113
107 Possessives 115
108 Adjectives 117
109 Adverbs 119
110 Adjectives as Complements 121

111 Compound Subjects 123
112 Compound Predicates 125
113 Compound Complements 127
114 Compound Sentences 129
115 Diagramming Practice 131
116 More Diagramming Practice 133

HANDBOOK OF TERMS 135

Name .... Date ....

1 Sentences

A **sentence** is a group of words that expresses a complete thought. Every sentence has a **subject** (a person, a place, a thing, or an idea) and a **predicate** (an action or a state of being).

SUBJECT	PREDICATE
George Washington and his wife	**lived at Mount Vernon.**

SUBJECT	PREDICATE
His wife's name	**was Martha.**

Read each example. Write *S* on the line if the words form a sentence. Put a period at the end of each sentence.

_____ 1. George Washington had a large farm in Virginia

_____ 2. Tobacco and wheat

_____ 3. Washington raised horses and cattle

_____ 4. Once he even owned a buffalo

_____ 5. The farm had a flour mill and a blacksmith shop

_____ 6. Workers on the farm made cloth, shoes, and barrels

_____ 7. A peach and an apple orchard

_____ 8. Some supplies had to be ordered from England

_____ 9. Farm implements, tools, paint, hats, and silk stockings

_____ 10. "Buy nothing you can make yourselves," Washington said

George Washington believed in being self-sufficient. Write three sentences with examples of things you are able to do without help from others.

Name .... Date ....

2 Statements and Questions

Telling sentences are called **statements.** A statement ends with a period.

George Washington owned a large farm.

Asking sentences are called **questions.** A question ends with a question mark.

Do you know the name of his farm?

Every sentence begins with a capital letter.

Sentences

A **Put a period at the end of each statement and a question mark at the end of each question.**

1. Have you ever been on a farm
2. There are many jobs to do on a farm
3. Everybody in the family helps
4. What kinds of jobs do farmers do
5. Some farmers grow fruits, vegetables, or grains
6. Farmers have to water their crops
7. Other farmers raise animals
8. Farm children help feed the animals
9. Do you think it is harder to raise crops or animals
10. Why is a farmer's work important

B **Make statements and questions by matching the words in Column A with the words in Column B. Write the correct letter on the line.**

COLUMN A	COLUMN B
1. Cotton ________	a. raise cotton?
2. Why do farmers ________	b. grow best?
3. People ________	c. need a lot of sun.
4. Where does cotton ________	d. is a plant.
5. Cotton plants ________	e. use cotton to make clothes.

Name .... Date ....

3 Question Words

A **question** often starts with a question word. Some question words are *who, what, when, where, why,* and *how.*

Complete each question with *who, what, when, where, why,* or *how*. Remember to start each sentence with a capital letter.

1. A lot of wheat is grown in South Dakota.
   ______________ is a lot of wheat grown?
2. Wheat grows well there because the soil is rich.
   ______________ does wheat grow well there?
3. Wheat farmers plow the fields carefully.
   ______________ do wheat farmers plow the fields?
4. Then the farmers plant the wheat seeds.
   ______________ plants the wheat seeds?
5. The wheat plants start to grow in the fall.
   ______________ starts to grow in the fall?
6. Snow protects the young plants from cold temperatures.
   ______________ protects the young plants from cold temperatures?
7. During the spring the snow melts.
   ______________ does the snow melt?
8. The melted snow waters the wheat plants.
   ______________ waters the wheat plants?
9. In the summer the wheat is harvested.
   ______________ is the wheat harvested?
10. People everywhere eat foods made from wheat flour.
    ______________ eats foods made from wheat flour?

Sentences

Name .... Date ....

4 Commands

A **command** is a sentence that tells what to do. The subject of a command is *you*, but the subject is not stated in most commands. A command ends with a period.

Open your book.

Read how to do the experiment.

Change each sentence into a command.

1. You can find out how a plant grows toward light.

   ____

2. First you should put a little soil into two old saucers.

   ____

3. Next you should plant three beans on each saucer.

   ____

4. Then you must water the beans so that the soil is moist.

   ____

5. Now you need to find a small box with a lid.

   ____

6. You should cut a small hole in one side of the box.

   ____

7. You must place one saucer in the box and put the lid on the box.

   ____

8. You have to leave the other saucer in the open.

   ____

9. You should water the plants as needed.

   ____

10. You should observe the plants every day to see how they grow.

    ____

Name .... Date ....

5 Exclamations

An **exclamation** is a sentence that expresses strong or sudden emotion. It ends with an exclamation point.

She deserves a big thank-you!

Put the correct punctuation mark (an exclamation point, a period, or a question mark) at the end of each sentence.

1. Have you heard of Jane Addams
2. She was born in 1860
3. She wanted to be a doctor, but she wasn't healthy enough
4. In 1888 she moved to Chicago
5. Many people in the city were very poor
6. Living conditions were horrible
7. Addams wanted to help, so she started Hull House
8. What was Hull House
9. It was a place where people could go to get help
10. Hull House had a library and an employment office
11. Adults could go to school there at night
12. Addams started the city's first kindergarten there
13. The results of her work were amazing
14. How was Addams rewarded for her work against war
15. She was the first American woman to receive the Nobel Peace Prize

Jane Addams worked hard to help people in need. Give an example of how you could help someone in need.

Name .... Date ....

6 Kinds of Sentences

A sentence can be a **statement,** a **question,** a **command,** or an **exclamation.**

A **Put the correct punctuation mark at the end of each sentence.**

1. A neighborhood is a place where people live
2. What is your neighborhood like
3. A community can be made up of neighborhoods
4. A big community has houses, stores, restaurants, and schools
5. A city is made up of many communities
6. What can you find in a city
7. Most cities have offices, stores, and theaters
8. Cities can be really busy
9. A city has factories and parks
10. Would you rather live in a city or on a farm

B **Decide whether each sentence is a statement, a question, a command, or an exclamation. Write your answer on the line.**

______________ 1. There are many good restaurants in my community.

______________ 2. Have you ever eaten Thai food?

______________ 3. I like it better than any other food!

______________ 4. My favorite Thai restaurant is House of Pho.

______________ 5. Go there to try it as soon as you can.

______________ 6. Do you like Mexican food?

______________ 7. Tony's Tacos is near here.

______________ 8. Tony makes the greatest tacos in town!

______________ 9. Eat at Tony's Tacos.

______________ 10. Tacos are delicious!

Sentences

Name .... Date ....

7 Subjects

A sentence has a subject and a predicate. The **subject** is who or what the sentence is about. The **simple subject** is usually a noun. It names the person, place, or thing that is talked about. The **complete subject** is the simple subject and any words that describe it.

SENTENCE	**Many wild animals live in national parks.**
COMPLETE SUBJECT	**Many wild animals**
SIMPLE SUBJECT	**animals**

Sentences

A **Whom or what is each sentence about? Underline the complete subject of each sentence.**

1. Three tall giraffes eat leaves from the trees.
2. A baby gorilla sleeps in its mother's arms.
3. The sleek brown otters slid down the riverbank.
4. A large male lion roared loudly.
5. The chattering monkeys swing from branches.
6. A big black bear scratched its back on a tree trunk.
7. Two zookeepers were giving an elephant a shower.
8. A family of zebras rested in the shade.
9. The huge hippopotamus lay in a pond.
10. The excited children are watching the seals.

B **Write the simple subject that best fits each sentence on the line.**

canary colt dog fish kitten

1. The little gray ______________ is licking its whiskers.
2. A frisky ______________ galloped across the field.
3. The ______________ is singing in its cage.
4. The big brown ______________ caught the stick.
5. My ______________ swim in their bowl.

Name .... Date ....

8 Predicates

A sentence has a subject and a predicate. The **predicate** tells what the subject is or does. The **simple predicate** is a verb, a word or words that name an action or a state of being. The **complete predicate** is the simple predicate and any words that describe it.

SENTENCE	**Washington, D.C.,**	**is an exciting city.**
COMPLETE PREDICATE		**is an exciting city**
SIMPLE PREDICATE		**is**
SENTENCE	**The president**	**lives in Washington, D.C.**
COMPLETE PREDICATE		**lives in Washington, D.C.**
SIMPLE PREDICATE		**lives**

A **Underline the complete predicate in each sentence.**

1. A city can be a noisy place.
2. Airplanes roar loudly overhead.
3. Huge buses rumble to bus stops.
4. Traffic police blow their whistles.
5. Some workers wear earplugs to protect their hearing.

B **Draw a circle around the simple predicate in each sentence.**

1. A community provides goods and services.
2. Restaurants and stores sell goods.
3. Police departments and fire departments supply services.
4. Everyone in a community shares the goods and the services.
5. Customers buy tickets for the movies.
6. People take taxis to the airport.
7. Doctors and nurses help sick people.
8. Workers in factories make cars and trucks.
9. Children and teachers study in the library.
10. Mail carriers deliver packages.

Name .... Date ....

9 Combining Predicates

If two sentences have the same subject, the sentences can be combined to make one sentence with one subject and two predicates. A sentence that has two predicates has a **compound predicate.**

Two sentences with the same subject and different predicates
Michael poured the water. Michael added the ice.

Combining sentences, using *and* to connect the predicates
Michael poured the water and added the ice.

Sentences

A Underline the complete predicates in each sentence.

1. Astronomers look at planets and study the stars.
2. Chemists experiment with solids and mix liquids.
3. Geologists explore the earth and examine rocks.
4. Botanists discover new plants and give them names.
5. Zoologists watch wildlife in nature and write reports.

B Each pair of sentences has the same subject. Combine each pair to make one smooth sentence.

1. Machines make work easier. Machines help get more work done.

   ____

2. A pulley is attached to the flagpole. A pulley helps raise the flag.

   ____

3. A lever needs a fulcrum. A lever requires force.

   ____

4. Wheels turn. Wheels sometimes squeak.

   ____

5. Machines are used every day. Machines work in different ways.

   ____

Name .... Date ....

10 Combining Subjects

If two sentences have the same predicate, the sentences can be combined to make one sentence with two subjects and one predicate. A sentence with two subjects has a **compound subject.**

Two sentences with different subjects and the same predicate

Diane searched the Internet. Kevin searched the Internet.

Combining sentences, using *and* to connect the subjects

Diane and Kevin searched the Internet.

Sentences

Each pair of sentences has the same predicate. Combine each pair to make one smooth sentence.

1. Ashley thought about possible topics. Pat thought about possible topics.

____

2. Karol investigated swimming. Jack investigated swimming.

____

3. Claire did the research. Royce did the research.

____

4. Mari wrote the first draft. Eileen wrote the first draft.

____

5. Neil edited the story. Evan edited the story.

____

6. José typed the second draft. Elise typed the second draft.

____

7. Jay enjoyed doing the writing. Alice enjoyed doing the writing.

____

8. Lee added pictures to the report. Cheryl added pictures to the report.

____

9. Karly drew graphs for the report. Jojo drew graphs for the report.

____

10. Ms. Cardy eagerly read the report. The parents eagerly read the report.

Name .... Date ....

11 Combining Sentences

Short sentences about similar ideas are sometimes boring to read. Combine short sentences into one longer sentence, using a comma and the word *and, but,* or *or.* When two sentences are combined into one sentence with a connecting word, the sentence is called a **compound sentence.**

The children planted flowers. Their father watered the lawn.

The children planted flowers, and their father watered the lawn.

Use a comma and the word *and, but,* or *or* to combine each pair of short sentences.

1. Andy cut the grass. Abbey collected the clippings.

   ____

2. Ann trimmed the bushes. Mary weeded the flower bed.

   ____

3. Flowers are planted around the tree. A fence keeps the rabbits away.

   ____

4. A bird feeder is in the maple tree. A squirrel eats the birdseed.

   ____

5. Carrots grow near the gate. Raspberries grow along the fence.

   ____

6. The evergreen grew more than one foot. The oak tree grew six inches.

   ____

7. We ate lunch. Our parents took a nap.

   ____

8. I hike in the forest. I walk along the beach.

   ____

9. A turtle sat on a log. A duck landed on the pond.

   ____

10. The sky was bright blue. The afternoon sun was warm.

   ____

Name .... Date ....

12 Avoiding Run-on Sentences

A **run-on sentence** is one in which two or more sentences are put together without the proper connector. Some run-on sentences are separated by only a comma. Those run-ons can easily be fixed by adding *and, but,* or *or* after the comma.

RUN-ON SENTENCE	**Some deserts are very hot, many kinds of animals live there.**
COMPOUND SENTENCE	**Some deserts are very hot, but many kinds of animals live there.**

Decide whether each sentence is a run-on or a correctly combined sentence. If it is a run-on, rewrite it as a compound sentence.

1. Cactus wrens live in thorny shrubs, they eat mostly insects.

____

2. These wrens can run quickly, they usually fly.

____

3. Their nests are lined with feathers or fur, they have long entrances.

____

4. Gila monsters find shade under rocks, or they dig burrows.

____

5. The desert tortoise lives in sandy deserts, it can live 50 to 80 years.

____

6. This tortoise has a hard upper shell, and its tail is very short.

____

7. The female tortoise digs a shallow pit, she lays her eggs in it.

____

8. She covers the eggs with sand, then she abandons them.

____

9. A roadrunner has short wings, it rarely flies.

____

10. A roadrunner runs from its enemies, or it crouches and hides.

____

Name .... Date ....

13 Reviewing Sentences

A **Read each example. Write *S* on the line if the words form a sentence. Put a period at the end of each sentence.**

_____ 1. Mrs. Chase's class took a trip to Washington, D.C., in the spring

_____ 2. They went to the Smithsonian Institution Building

_____ 3. The red castle on the mall

_____ 4. A collection of museums

_____ 5. Everyone enjoyed the visit

B **Read each sentence. Write *E* on the line if the sentence is an exclamation. Write *Q* on the line if the sentence is a question. Put the correct punctuation mark at the end of each sentence.**

_____ 6. Did the students enjoy the National Air and Space Museum

_____ 7. The old airplanes were amazing

_____ 8. The spaceship was awesome

_____ 9. Did they see the lunar vehicles

_____ 10. Are they going on a trip again next year

C **Complete each question with *who, what, when, where, why,* or *how.***

11. They saw Owney the dog at the National Postal Museum.

    _______________ did they see Owney?

12. Several authors wrote books about Owney.

    _______________ wrote books about Owney?

13. The National Museum of American History is closed on Mondays.

    _______________ is the National Museum of American History closed?

14. The Hope Diamond is a huge blue diamond.

    _______________ is the name of that huge blue diamond?

15. The diamond can be seen in the National Museum of Natural History.

    _______________ can the diamond be seen?

Sentences

Continued →

Name .... Date ....

D **Read each sentence. Draw a line to separate the subject and the predicate.**

16. Chicago is the third-largest city in the United States.
17. Thousands of tourists visit Chicago every week.
18. Famous architects designed many of the buildings in Chicago.
19. The Architecture Foundation offers tours of downtown landmarks.
20. Wrigley Field is a popular place in the summer.
21. Baseball fans love to watch games there.
22. Navy Pier is another favorite spot for tourists.
23. People walk, bike, or skate along the lakefront.
24. A Ferris wheel, a children's museum, and a theater attract crowds.
25. A big-city vacation can be a lot of fun!

Try It Yourself

Write four sentences about the place where you live. Be sure each sentence expresses a complete thought. Use correct punctuation.

____

____

____

____

Check Your Own Work

Choose a piece of writing from your writing portfolio, a work in progress, an assignment from another class, or a letter. Revise it, using the skills you have reviewed. This checklist will help you.

- ✔ Does each sentence express a complete thought?
- ✔ Does each sentence start with a capital letter?
- ✔ Does each sentence end with the correct punctuation mark?

Name .... Date ....

14 Nouns

A **noun** is a word that names a person, a place, or a thing.

PERSON	PLACE	THING
Meriwether Lewis	**Montana**	**trail**

A **Decide if the noun in the first column is a person, a place, or a thing. Circle the correct answer.**

1. boat	person	place	thing
2. Thomas Jefferson	person	place	thing
3. journals	person	place	thing
4. William Clark	person	place	thing
5. St. Louis, Missouri	person	place	thing

B **Underline the nouns in each sentence.**

1. President Thomas Jefferson sent Lewis and Clark to explore the West.
2. Lewis and Clark began the trip in a town named St. Louis, Missouri.
3. They made a journey across the Great Plains and the Rocky Mountains.
4. Lewis and Clark were helped by Sacagawea, a Native American woman.
5. The journals of Lewis and Clark tell the story of the trip.

LEWIS

Lewis and Clark braved many hardships as they explored the West. Write three sentences describing a time when you overcame hardships to complete something. Underline the nouns.

CLARK

Nouns

 Level C

Name .... Date ....

15 Proper Nouns and Common Nouns

A **proper noun** names a particular person, place, or thing.

A **common noun** names any one member of a group of persons, places, or things.

PROPER NOUN	COMMON NOUN
Mrs. Buehl	**librarian**

Nouns

Read each sentence. Circle each proper noun and underline each common noun.

1. My friends like to go to the Denver Public Library.
2. They check out new books every Friday.
3. Kim and Karen read mainly mysteries.
4. Their favorite mystery is *The Boxcar Children.*
5. Jim reads many books by his favorite author, Roald Dahl.
6. Mr. Fuentes, the librarian, helps Jim search the catalog.
7. Almost instantly Jim can see a list of books by Dahl.
8. Joan likes books by Laura Ingalls Wilder and Frances Hodgson Burnett.
9. Burnett wrote the book *The Secret Garden.*
10. The book is about a girl named Mary Lennox.
11. Mary finds a hidden garden at Misselthwaite Manor in the countryside.
12. The public library has many interesting things to do.
13. Malik likes to rent CDs and movies from the library.
14. Jim and Kiera like to perform plays for story time.
15. Many libraries have newspapers from other cities.

Name .... Date ....

16 Singular Nouns and Plural Nouns

A **singular noun** names one person, place, or thing. A **plural noun** names more than one person, place, or thing.

The plural of most nouns is formed by adding *-s* to the singular.

computer **computers** **book** **books**

The plural of nouns ending in *s, x, z, ch,* and *sh* is formed by adding *-es* to the singular.

dish **dishes** **beach** **beaches**

Nouns

A **Write the plural form of each noun.**

1. bench ____________
2. nugget ____________
3. glass ____________
4. waltz ____________
5. church ____________
6. brick ____________
7. icicle ____________
8. peach ____________
9. giraffe ____________
10. dash ____________

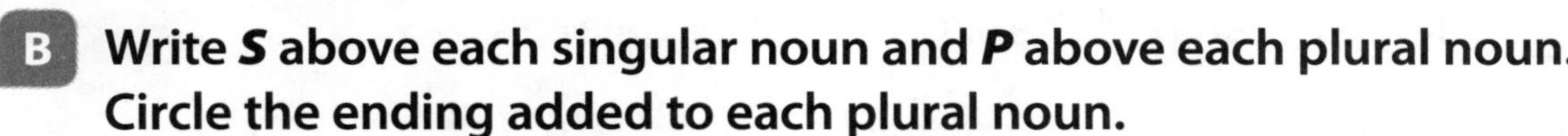

B **Write *S* above each singular noun and *P* above each plural noun. Circle the ending added to each plural noun.**

One day a fox was walking in the forest when he spotted several bunches of grapes hanging from a vine. After jumping several times, he managed to reach a large bunch. He carried the fruit toward his den.

As the fox passed a lake, he looked down into the water. There was another fox carrying another bunch of grapes. He couldn't believe that two foxes could be so lucky. He wanted both bunches! When he opened his mouth to grab the second bunch, though, his own grapes fell into the water and disappeared! So the greedy animal had no supper that night.

Name .... Date ....

17 More Plural Nouns

To make most nouns plural, you add *-s* or *-es* to the singular form. Some nouns that end in *y* are different. To form the plural of a noun ending in a consonant followed by *y*, change the *y* to *i* and add *-es*.

baby	**babies**	**puppy**	**puppies**
city	**cities**	**party**	**parties**

For nouns ending in a vowel and *y*, just add *-s*.

boy	**boys**	**key**	**keys**
ray	**rays**	**toy**	**toys**

A **Underline the nouns in each sentence. Write *S* above each singular noun and *P* above each plural noun.**

1. My hobbies include collecting stuffed toys.
2. The puppies are sleeping among the daisies.
3. The boys are catching guppies in the pond.
4. The scientist searched the skies for other galaxies.
5. We picked cherries and strawberries at the farm.

B **Write the plural form for each noun.**

1. bunny ____________
2. joy ____________
3. library ____________
4. valley ____________
5. firefly ____________
6. country ____________
7. factory ____________
8. story ____________
9. bay ____________
10. copy ____________
11. day ____________
12. diary ____________
13. memory ____________
14. chimney ____________
15. lady ____________
16. dairy ____________
17. play ____________
18. berry ____________
19. guy ____________
20. jay ____________

Name .... Date ....

18 Irregular Plural Nouns

The plurals of some nouns look different from their singular forms. **Irregular plural nouns** do not end in *s* or *es*.

ox	**oxen**	**child**	**children**
tooth	**teeth**	**foot**	**feet**
mouse	**mice**	**woman**	**women**
goose	**geese**	**man**	**men**

Some nouns have the same form in the plural and in the singular.

sheep	**sheep**	**deer**	**deer**
trout	**trout**	**moose**	**moose**

A **If the noun is singular, write *S* on the line. If the noun is plural, write *P*. If the noun can be singular or plural, write *SP*.**

______ 1. children ______ 6. ox

______ 2. deer ______ 7. men

______ 3. mouse ______ 8. sheep

______ 4. teeth ______ 9. fish

______ 5. feet ______ 10. geese

B **Complete each sentence with the plural of the noun in parentheses.**

1. Farmers raise ________________ for meat and wool. (sheep)
2 They raise ________________ for meat and feathers. (goose)
3. Some farmers used to use ________________ to pull plows. (ox)
4. Several kinds of ________________ are raised on farms. (salmon)
5. Cats chase ________________ from farmers' barns. (mouse)
6. Those ________________ are veterinarians. (man)
7. They are checking the horse's ________________. (foot)
8. They will also check its ________________. (tooth)
9. These ______________ are studying wildlife. (woman)
10. They want to keep ______________ from eating the crops. (deer)

Nouns

Name .... Date ....

19 Singular Possessive Nouns

A **singular possessive noun** shows that one person or thing possesses, or owns, something. To form the singular possessive, add an apostrophe and the letter *s* (-*'s*) to a singular noun.

NOUN	SINGULAR POSSESSIVE NOUN
baker	**baker's oven**
Zach	**Zach's trophy**

A **Circle the possessive noun in each sentence.**

1. Dad's garden is full of tomatoes, onions, and cilantro.
2. My mom's recipe for salsa calls for all those ingredients.
3. First she cuts up about three of Dad's garden tomatoes.
4. She makes sure the knife's blade is sharp, so that it cuts easily.
5. Second she dices an onion and puts it into Aunt Cele's favorite bowl.
6. My father's cilantro will taste great in the salsa.
7. Next I mix the ingredients with a little salt and pepper before adding Mr. Black's award-winning jalapeño peppers.
8. My sister's friend is able to eat an entire jalapeño pepper.
9. Teresa's tongue hurts when the pepper seeds touch it.
10. I plan to make this salsa for our town's Mexican fiesta next week.

B **Rewrite each group of words, making the italicized noun a possessive noun.**

EXAMPLE
the nose of the *clown* ____the clown's nose____

1. the recipe of the *chef* ________________
2. the plate of the *customer* ________________
3. the meal of the *president* ________________
4. the laughter from the *guest* ________________
5. the cookie of the *child* ________________

Nouns

Name .... Date ....

20 Plural Possessive Nouns

A **plural possessive noun** shows that more than one person or thing owns something. To form the plural possessive of most nouns, change the singular noun into a plural noun and add an apostrophe (') after the *s* of the plural form.

SINGULAR	PLURAL	PLURAL POSSESSIVE
boy	**boys**	**boys' toys**
bench	**benches**	**benches' legs**

A **Write the plural form and the plural possessive form of each noun.**

	PLURAL	PLURAL POSSESSIVE
1. hen	______________	______________
2. mother	______________	______________
3. factory	______________	______________
4. hiker	______________	______________
5. church	______________	______________
6. student	______________	______________
7. teacher	______________	______________
8. puppy	______________	______________
9. musician	______________	______________
10. watch	______________	______________

B **Complete each sentence with the plural possessive form of the noun in parentheses.**

1. My ______________ hobby is raising rabbits. (brother)
2. The ______________ homes are in the backyard. (rabbit)
3. Their ______________ floors are warm and dry. (hutch)
4. The ______________ ears wiggle. (bunny)
5. The ______________ pets are happy. (boy)

Name .... Date ....

21 Irregular Plural Possessive Nouns

The plural forms of irregular nouns do not end in *s*. To form the plural possessive of irregular nouns, change the singular noun into a plural noun and add an apostrophe and the letter *s (-'s)* to the plural form.

SINGULAR	PLURAL	PLURAL POSSESSIVE
man	**men**	**men's**
goose	**geese**	**geese's**
woman	**women**	**women's**

A **Write the plural form and the plural possessive form of each noun.**

	PLURAL	PLURAL POSSESSIVE
1. mouse	____________	____________
2. baby	____________	____________
3. child	____________	____________
4. deer	____________	____________
5. salmon	____________	____________
6. tooth	____________	____________
7. snowman	____________	____________
8. sheep	____________	____________
9. foot	____________	____________
10. ox	____________	____________

B **Rewrite each group of words. Insert apostrophes to show plural possession. Be careful. Some nouns are regular plurals, and some nouns are irregular plurals.**

EXAMPLE
salmons fins ____ salmon's fins ____

1. deers antlers ____________
2. blue jays nests ____________
3. libraries computers ____________
4. sheeps wool ____________
5. childrens game ____________

Nouns

Name .... Date ....

22 Singular Possessive Nouns and Plural Possessive Nouns

A Each of these sentences contains at least one possessive noun. Read each sentence. Underline each singular possessive noun and circle each plural possessive noun.

1. Everyone likes to work in Ms. Price's school store.
2. Ali's job is to stock the store with paper, pencils, erasers, and other supplies.
3. Jane takes the students' orders and fills them.
4. Robert takes each child's money and gives change if necessary.
5. The workers have the principal's and the teachers' trust that they will operate the store properly.

B Complete each sentence with the singular possessive of the noun given.

dog 1. The ______________ bark was worse than its bite.

Anna 2. ______________ paints spilled onto the floor.

snake 3. I saw the ______________ forked tongue.

Josh 4. ______________ firefighter hat had a light on it.

man 5. The ______________ glasses were too big for him.

C Complete each sentence with the plural possessive of the noun given.

clown 1. The ______________ costumes were bright yellow and green.

woman 2. Did you find the ______________ department?

lawyer 3. All of the ______________ offices are on the fifth floor.

shark 4. I don't want to see any ______________ teeth.

veterinarian 5. ______________ patients might have fur, hair, scales, or feathers.

Nouns

Name .... Date ....

23 Collective Nouns

A noun that names a group of things or people is called a **collective noun.**

audience	**club**	**flock**	**pack**
army	**crew**	**group**	**pair**
band	**crowd**	**herd**	**swarm**
class	**family**	**litter**	**team**

A collective noun usually goes with an action word that ends in *s* in the present tense.

The crowd roars.

Our class takes field trips.

A **Underline the collective noun or nouns in each sentence.**

1. The scout troop is camping in the woods.
2. A flock of sheep is in the field.
3. The crew hauled up the sails.
4. My dog had a litter of puppies.
5. My family went to hear the band play.
6. Our club visited a farm that had a colony of bees.
7. The audience stood and cheered for the team.
8. I couldn't see over the crowd.
9. A group of scientists watched the pack of wolves.
10. That farmer owns a herd of cattle.

B **Complete each sentence with a collective noun from the list above.**

1. My soccer ____________ won the game!
2. Julio plays guitar in a ____________.
3. A ____________ of geese flew over the pond.
4. The art ____________ made posters for the concert.
5. This kitten is the cutest one in the ____________.

Name .... Date ....

24 Nouns as Subjects

A noun may be used as the subject of a sentence. The **subject** tells what the sentence is about. It tells who or what does something.

Janet rubbed the dog's ears.

The dog wagged its tail.

A Look at each sentence. Underline each noun that is a subject.

1. Kim pointed to the old house.
2. A light bobbed past the window.
3. Shadows flickered on the curtains.
4. Tall trees shaded the porch.
5. The wind rustled the leaves.
6. The children huddled on the sidewalk.
7. Yan climbed the steps and rang the bell.
8. The door opened slowly.
9. A woman called, "Who's there?"
10. Kenny yelled, "Trick or treat!"

B Complete each sentence with a noun. You may add other words such as *a* or *the.*

1. ______________________________ ran across the field.
2. ______________________________ floated in the sky.
3. ______________________________ took some sandwiches out of the basket.
4. ______________________________ tasted delicious.
5. ______________________________ watched everything that happened.

Nouns

Name .... Date ....

25 Words Used as Nouns and Verbs

Many words can be used both as nouns and as verbs. In the first sentence, *copy* is used as a noun. In the second sentence, it is used as a verb.

Please print a copy of the letter.

Copy these sentences on your paper.

If the underlined word is a noun, write *N* on the line. If it is a verb, write *V* on the line.

______ 1. I think I passed the test.

______ 2. Please test the batteries in the smoke alarm.

______ 3. Kangaroos leap high.

______ 4. The dog made a leap for the stick.

______ 5. The scout troop often puts on plays.

______ 6. My kitten plays with her catnip mouse.

______ 7. Would you bait my hook?

______ 8. We're using worms for bait.

______ 9. The audience claps for the performers.

______ 10. There were two loud claps of thunder.

______ 11. Let's vote for the smartest person.

______ 12. Nico cast his vote for Keith.

______ 13. Hand me the hammer and the nails.

______ 14. The nails on his right hand are dirty.

______ 15. The carpenter nails the boards together.

Name .... Date ....

26 Reviewing Nouns

A **Decide whether each noun is common or proper and if the noun names a person, a place, or a thing. Write *common* or *proper* on the first line. Write *person, place,* or *thing* on the second line.**

1. Daniel Boone ____________ ____________
2. spoons ____________ ____________
3. pencil ____________ ____________
4. library ____________ ____________
5. Miguel ____________ ____________
6. Jody's Diner ____________ ____________
7. carpenter ____________ ____________
8. Krispy Krunchy Fish ____________ ____________
9. flowers ____________ ____________
10. park ____________ ____________

B **Circle the collective noun in each sentence.**

11. The band will march in the parade.
12. My family helped look for the lost dog.
13. I hope our baseball team wins today.
14. A swarm of bees circled around a hive.
15. The audience cheered for the actors.

C **Write the plural form of each singular noun.**

16. cobweb	____________	21. toy	____________
17. house	____________	22. puppy	____________
18. mouse	____________	23. sheep	____________
19. goose	____________	24. lunch	____________
20. fox	____________	25. foot	____________

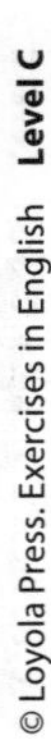

Continued →

Name .... Date ....

D **Rewrite each group of words, using a possessive noun.**

26. the books of Tom ____________________
27. the fur of the bunnies ____________________
28. the shoes of the boys ____________________
29. the web of the spider ____________________
30. the hats of the women ____________________

Try It Yourself

Write a sentence that contains each kind of noun listed.
Check for capital letters and the correct use of apostrophes.

Common Noun ____________________

Proper Noun ____________________

Collective Noun ____________________

Singular Possessive Noun ____________________

Plural Possessive Noun ____________________

Check Your Own Work

Choose a piece of writing from your writing portfolio, a work in progress, an assignment from another class, or a letter. Revise it, using the skills you have reviewed. This checklist will help you.

- ✔ Have you capitalized all proper nouns?
- ✔ Have you used apostrophes to show ownership?
- ✔ In each plural possessive, is the apostrophe in the right place?

Name .... Date ....

27 Singular Pronouns

A **personal pronoun** is a word that takes the place of a noun. A **singular personal pronoun** refers to one person, place, or thing. The singular personal pronouns are *I, me, mine, you, yours, he, him, his, she, her, hers, it,* and *its.*

The cat jumped down from the roof.

It jumped down from the roof.

The flowers were for Carol.

The flowers were for her.

Pronouns

Write on the line the pronoun that takes the place of the word or words in italics.

______ 1. *Laura Ingalls* was born in the big woods of Wisconsin.

______ 2. *Ingalls* wrote a popular series of books.

______ 3. *Ingalls* wrote about life in a pioneer family in the late 1800s.

______ 4. Ingalls and her sisters called *their father* Pa.

______ 5. *Pa* took the family from Wisconsin to Kansas in a covered wagon.

______ 6. Grasshoppers destroyed *the wheat crop* one year.

______ 7. A hard winter of blizzards kept *Ingalls* inside from October to May.

______ 8. *Ingalls* worked as a teacher 12 miles from home.

______ 9. Laura Ingalls married *Almanzo Wilder.*

______ 10. *Life* was difficult on the prairie.

Laura Ingalls Wilder had courage throughout her hard life on the prairie. Using personal pronouns, write about a situation in which you showed courage.

Name .... Date ....

28 Plural Pronouns

A **plural personal pronoun** refers to more than one person, place, or thing.

The plural personal pronouns are *we, us, ours, they, them, theirs, you,* and *yours.* *You* and *yours* can be plural or singular.

Mom and Dad went to the bakery.

They went to the bakery.

A **Circle the plural pronoun or plural pronouns in each sentence.**

1. They ate bagels for breakfast.
2. We put strawberry jelly on the bagels.
3. The toasted sesame bagel was for them.
4. Can you two share the cream cheese with each other?
5. Are the cinnamon bagels for us?
6. We love to put butter and honey on bagels.
7. Mom gave us the knife for the butter.
8. Todd and Scott, do you work at the bakery?
9. They came late to breakfast.
10. We saved some bagels for them.

B **Write on the line a pronoun to take the place of the words in italics.**

__________ 1. *Carl and I* didn't understand the problem.

__________ 2. Will someone explain the answer to *Sheila and me?*

__________ 3. Mrs. Bosnak gave *you and Kiya* some help with the problem.

__________ 4. I'm glad the teacher didn't ask *Joel and Harry* to solve the problem.

__________ 5. *Most students* did the problem yesterday.

Name .... Date ....

29 Subject Pronouns

Some personal pronouns may be used as the subjects of sentences. Those pronouns are called **subject pronouns.** The subject pronouns are *I, we, you, he, she, it,* and *they*.

We liked the video.

She bought a skirt.

A **Circle the correct subject pronoun in each sentence.**

1. (Us We) expect company today.
2. (He Him) fixed the clock so it would work again.
3. Dad and (her she) will take the food to the picnic table.
4. (Them They) are going on a field trip.
5. (We Us) went horseback riding on the farm.
6. Carol and (I me) played checkers with Bruce.
7. (They Them) watched the parade go by.
8. (He Him) slid down the hill on a sled.
9. Shawn and (I me) raced to the beach.
10. (Her She) missed the train.

B **Write on the first line a subject pronoun to take the place of the word or words in italics. On the second line write *S* if the pronoun is singular or *P* if it is plural.**

	PRONOUN	*S* OR *P*
1. Dad said, "*Mom and Sue* should shop at the Big T."	________	________
2. *Sue* showed Mom a robot at the store.	________	________
3. *The robot* was on sale.	________	________
4. "*Dad* would like the robot," Sue said.	________	________
5. *Sue's mother and Sue* decided to buy it for him.	________	________

Name .... Date ....

30 Object Pronouns

Some personal pronouns may be used after the verb in a sentence. They are called **object pronouns.** The object pronouns are *me, us, you, him, her, it,* and *them*.

Dad promised me an ice-cream cone.

Greg sent her a thank-you note.

A **Circle the correct pronoun in parentheses. On the line write an *S* if the pronoun is singular or *P* if it is plural.**

______ 1. Mother gave (we us) pasta.

______ 2. We ate (they it) with delight.

______ 3. It was the same kind of pasta that Mom gave (we you), Anthony.

______ 4. Mother feeds (he him) well.

______ 5. Anthony loves (she her) for it.

______ 6. Mother likes fruit and thinks dinner should end with (him it).

______ 7. Mother makes baked apples and gives them to (we us).

______ 8. Vittorio and I taste (they them) with delight.

______ 9. By the end of dinner, there are many dishes in front of (I me).

______ 10. I offered to wash (they them).

B **On the line write an object pronoun that takes the place of the word or words in italics.**

______ 1. I asked *Tom* to hold the sunscreen.

______ 2. Lisa told *Tom and Jake* to put some of it on.

______ 3. Tom and Jake saved enough sunscreen for *Lisa and me*.

______ 4. The sun burned *Jake* anyway.

______ 5. Jake told *Lisa* that the sunburn really hurt.

Pronouns

Name .... Date ....

31 Possessive Pronouns

Possessive pronouns show who or what owns something. A possessive pronoun takes the place of a noun. The possessive pronouns are *mine, ours, yours, his, hers, its,* and *theirs*.

NOUN	POSSESSIVE PRONOUN
my hat	**mine**
their house	**theirs**

A **Match the object owned in Column A with the correct possessive pronoun in Column B. Write the letter on the line. Some possessive pronouns are used more than once.**

	COLUMN A	COLUMN B
_____	1. my house	a. yours
_____	2. the scooter's tire	b. ours
_____	3. your kitten	c. mine
_____	4. Tom's bike	d. theirs
_____	5. Megan and Josh's boat	e. his
_____	6. my family's cabin	f. hers
_____	7. Miss Tower's lawn	g. its
_____	8. Mr. Allen's motorcycle	
_____	9. your vacation	
_____	10. the children's toys	

B **Complete each sentence with a possessive pronoun: *mine, ours, yours, his, hers,* or *theirs.* Do not use the same pronoun in every sentence.**

1. Where are ______________?
2. I took ______________ by mistake.
3. ______________ are worn out.
4. Take ______________ to the library.
5. The polka dots on ______________ are green and yellow.

Pronouns

Name .... Date ....

32 Possessive Adjectives

An adjective is a word that describes a noun. *My, our, your, his, her, its,* and *their* are adjectives that go before nouns to show ownership. They are called **possessive adjectives.**

I lost my sunscreen.

Did you bring your beach ball?

A Circle the possessive adjective in each sentence.

1. Our family took a trip to the lake.
2. I wore my new swimsuit.
3. Laura brought her sunglasses.
4. Dad carried his fishing pole.
5. Where's your hat, Mike?
6. Mike and Laura dipped their toes in the lake.
7. Its water was cool and inviting.
8. Mom and Dad, your towels are over here.
9. I caught my first fish.
10. We all enjoyed our afternoon.

B Complete each sentence with a possessive adjective.

1. Laura bought ____________ sunglasses at the mall.
2. Mike left ____________ hat in the car.
3. ____________ new swimsuit is blue.
4. Mom and Dad ate ____________ sandwiches.
5. We picked up ____________ trash before we left.

Pronouns

 Level C

Name .... Date ....

33 Agreement of Pronouns and Verbs

A subject and its verb must agree. When *he, she,* or *it* is the subject, add *-s* to the present tense form of the verb.

I like cats.	**She likes dogs.**
We raise horses.	**He raises cattle.**
They eat oats.	**It eats hay.**

A **Circle the verb that agrees with the subject pronoun.**

1. She (own owns) a horse.
2. They (train trains) the horse every day.
3. He (give gives) it oats and water.
4. We (watch watches) her ride.
5. It (trot trots) around the ring.
6. You (need needs) a firm grip to be a good rider.
7. I (ride rides) with her often.
8. She (win wins) prizes in shows.
9. They (award awards) them to the best riders.
10. He (feel feels) proud of her.

B **Complete each sentence with a subject pronoun. Be sure the subject pronoun and the verb agree.**

1. ____________ wash the car every Saturday.
2. ____________ wipes the windows.
3. ____________ clean the tires.
4. ____________ polishes the hood.
5. ____________ shines in the sun.

Pronouns

Name .... Date ....

34 *I* and *Me*

I is used as the subject of a sentence.

I is a subject pronoun.

Me is usually used after the verb.

Me is an object pronoun.

I love going to the aquarium.

Dad saw me wave.

Pronouns

A Circle the correct pronoun in parentheses.

1. Mom and (I   me) went to the supermarket.
2. Rita saw my mom and (I   me) shopping.
3. Mom asked (I   me) what I wanted for dinner.
4. (I   Me) wanted tacos and salad.
5. Mom told (I   me) to find the taco shells in aisle four.
6. (I   Me) asked whether we could have soda pop with dinner.
7. She told (I   me) that fruit juice would be better.
8. She asked (I   me) to get some fresh raspberries for dessert.
9. (I   Me) really liked the tacos my mom made.
10. (I   Me) said, "My mom and (I   me) are a good team!"

B Complete each sentence with *I* or *me*.

1. Terry called __________ yesterday after school.
2. He asked __________ to go for a bike ride.
3. __________ was glad to join him.
4. Terry asked __________ to meet him at the park.
5. Terry and __________ had a good time.

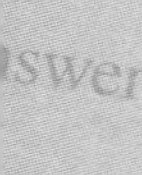

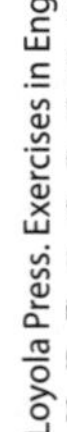

Name .... Date ....

35 Compound Subjects

Pronouns can be used in compound subjects. The subject pronouns are *I, you, he, she, it, we,* and *they.*

Mom, Dad, and I cleaned out the garage.

He and she moved their cars.

A Circle the correct pronoun or pronouns for each sentence.

1. Dad and (I me) made shelves for the cleaning supplies.
2. (He him) and Mom recycled the old newspapers.
3. Dylan and (her she) sorted all the sporting equipment.
4. (Them They) and Dad hung the tools on the wall.
5. Grace and (he him) put all the toys into bins.
6. (We Us) and Mom washed the windows.
7. (Her She) and Dad made a space for the gardening supplies.
8. (He Him) and (I me) swept the floor carefully.
9. (Us We) and the neighbors put our trash at the curb.
10. (They them) and (us we) were pleased.

B Complete each sentence with a subject pronoun or pronouns.

1. Mom and ____________ made potato salad.
2. ____________ and Brian set up the grill.
3. ____________ and ____________ washed the patio furniture.
4. ____________ and Dad started the fire.
5. ____________ and the neighbors grilled hamburgers.

Pronouns

Name .... Date ....

36 Compound Objects

Pronouns can be used as compound objects. The object pronouns are *me, you, him, her, it, us,* and *them.*

Rachel helped Mitch and me with the homework.

I showed him and her how to use fractions.

A Circle the correct pronoun or pronouns for each sentence.

1. Mrs. Harris hired Brad and (I me) to babysit her son and daughter.
2. We dressed (she her) and (he him) in warm clothes.
3. I pulled Brad and (them they) on a sled.
4. Brad showed (they them) and (I me) how to make snow angels.
5. We helped (him he) and (her she) make a snow fort.
6. Connie joined (them they) and (we us) in a snowball fight.
7. They hit (her she) and (us we) with snowballs.
8. We took (he him) and (her she) back home.
9. Mrs. Harris made (they them) and (us we) hot soup for lunch.
10. She paid Brad and (me I) for helping with the children.

B Complete each sentence with an object pronoun or pronouns.

1. Dad and Mom asked my friends and ____________ to rake the yard.
2. We've helped ____________ and ____________ before.
3. Dad showed Mike and ____________ the new rake.
4. He helped ____________ and ____________ put the leaves in a bag.
5. Mom thanked ____________ and ____________ for helping.

Pronouns

Name .... Date ....

37 Reviewing Pronouns

A **Circle the pronoun or pronouns in each sentence.**

1. We saw a small lizard.
2. It jumped to a rock near me.
3. She drew pictures of it.
4. We always carry them.
5. I drew some pictures of it too.

B **Name the subject pronoun that would take the place of the word or words in italics. Write your answer on the line.**

________ 6. *Melissa* plays the cello.

________ 7. *Joe and Beth* practice playing guitar together.

________ 8. *Billy* is learning a song to play on the piano.

________ 9. *Mara and I* prefer playing the trumpet to playing the tuba.

________ 10. *The tuba* is large and heavy.

C **Name a pronoun that would take the place of the word or words in italics that follow the verb. Write your answer on the line.**

________ 11. Put *the camera* on the tripod.

________ 12. Mom asked *Jeff and Betsy* to smile.

________ 13. Jeff told *Betsy* something funny.

________ 14. The camera wasn't pointing toward *Dad and me*.

________ 15. I took a picture of *Dad* at the top of the canyon.

Pronouns

Continued →

D **Underline the possessive pronoun or pronouns in each sentence.**

16. That book of folktales is his.
17. Carolyn's folktale came from the same country as mine.
18. Hers came from France.
19. Is yours an African folktale?
20. Theirs is more interesting than ours.

E **Complete each sentence with *I* or *me*.**

21. Keri and ______ read "The Shepherd and the Princess."
22. ______ enjoy reading folktales.
23. Keri told Colleen and ______ that "The Three Magi" was her favorite story.
24. Colleen asked ______ to read it to her.
25. ______ enjoyed reading it aloud.

Try It Yourself

Write three sentences about a book that you like or dislike. Use pronouns, including possessive pronouns. Be sure to use *I* and *me* correctly.

____

____

____

Check Your Own Work

Choose a piece of writing from your writing portfolio, a work in progress, an assignment for another class, or a letter. Revise it, using the skills you have reviewed. This checklist will help you.

- ✔ Have you used pronouns in place of nouns?
- ✔ Have you used possessive pronouns to show who owns something?
- ✔ Have you used *I* and *me* correctly?

Name .... Date ....

38 Verbs

A **verb** tells what someone or something does or what someone or something is.

The doctor talks with patients.

The shirt is blue and white.

Circle the verbs in the following sentences.

1. Agnes Gonxha Bojaxhiu joined a religious order in 1928.
2. She took the name of Teresa.
3. Then she moved to India.
4. Teresa worked as a history and geography teacher.
5. In a hospital there, she helped sick and hungry mothers.
6. Later she lived among the poorest of the poor people.
7. She started the Missionaries of Charity in India.
8. The Missionaries of Charity help people who are in need.
9. Mother Teresa died in September 1997.
10. Even now Mother Teresa's Missionaries of Charity continue her work around the world.

Mother Teresa dedicated her life to helping those who were poor. Write three sentences describing what you could do to help someone. Underline the verb in each sentence.

Verbs

Name .... Date ....

39 Action Verbs

Action verbs tell what someone or something does.

Fish swim. **Spiders spin.** **Artists paint.**

Read the poem. Use action verbs from the poem to complete the sentences below.

How Creatures Move
A lion walks on padded paws;
squirrels leap from limb to limb.
A crab runs with two pinchy claws,
and seals can dive and swim.
Some monkeys swing with twisty tails
high up in the trees,
and birds can spread their wings and sail
or hop on lawns with ease.
Boy and girls hop too, you know.
Kids all play games for fun.
Just like merry animals,
they leap and prance and run.

1. The lion __________ .
2. Squirrels __________ .
3. A crab __________ .
4. Seals can __________ and __________ .
5. Monkeys __________ .
6. Birds can __________ their wings and __________ among the treetops.
7. Birds may also __________ on the ground.
8. Boys and girls __________ too.
9. Kids __________ games for fun.
10. They __________ and __________ and __________ .

Name .... Date ....

40 More Action Verbs

Action verbs tell what someone or something does.

My aunt hikes in the mountains for exercise.

Roxanna reads a book every week.

A **Circle the action verbs in this story about a boy in Iowa.**

Andy lives on a farm in Iowa. His family raises dairy cows and grows corn. Andy's father milks the cows every morning and every evening. The family sells the milk to a dairy.

B **Complete each sentence with an action verb from the list. Use each verb once.**

live looks finds sail travels

1. Tara ____________________ at a map of the world.
2. She ____________________ Egypt on the map.
3. Tara ____________________ to Egypt to see her grandparents.
4. They ____________________ near the Nile River.
5. Boats ____________________ up and down this great river.

rides study sleep visit photographs

6. Tara and her grandparents ____________________ the great pyramids.
7. Tourists carefully ____________________ the pictures on the pyramid walls.
8. Grandfather ____________________ the Sphinx.
9. Grandmother ____________________ in the tour bus.
10. Tara and her grandparents ____________________ in a hotel.

Name .... Date ....

41 Being Verbs

A **being verb** shows what someone or something is. Being verbs do not express action. Some being verbs are *am, is, are, was, were, be, has been, had been, have been,* and *will be.*

Paulo and Ricardo are good at Internet searches.

Information about earthquakes is on the Internet.

A **Circle the verb in each sentence. On the line write *A* if the verb is an action verb or *B* if it is a being verb.**

_____ 1. Earthquakes are movements in plates of land.

_____ 2. We call a huge piece of land a *plate.*

_____ 3. Plates are like pieces of a large puzzle.

_____ 4. A fault line is a crack in the ground between two plates.

_____ 5. Pressure at fault lines causes earthquakes.

B **Put a check in front of each sentence that uses a being verb. Circle all being verbs.**

_____ 1. Earthquakes are possible in many parts of the world.

_____ 2. Landslides during earthquakes damage buildings, roads, and homes.

_____ 3. Fires start from broken fuel lines and electric cables.

_____ 4. California has been the site of many earthquakes.

_____ 5. The Richter scale measures the size and strength of earthquakes.

_____ 6. There is no way to stop an earthquake.

_____ 7. Scientists cannot predict earthquakes very well.

_____ 8. Earthquakes are dangerous natural events.

_____ 9. Tornadoes and hurricanes are also natural events.

_____ 10. Earthquakes will be a part of nature forever.

Verbs

Name .... Date ....

42 Helping Verbs

A verb can have more than one word. A **helping verb** is a verb added before the main verb to make the meaning clear. Some helping verbs are *am, is, are, was, were, be, been, do, does, has, have, had, will, can,* and *might.*

Our class has worked on many art projects.

The helping verb is *has*. The main verb is *worked*.

A Circle the helping verbs in each sentence.

1. Bernadette was working on a magnet experiment.
2. She is checking whether her magnet will attract paper clips through cardboard.
3. Magnetic fields were found surrounding planets.
4. My compass might have a magnet inside.
5. Electricity will turn a piece of iron wrapped in wire into a magnet.

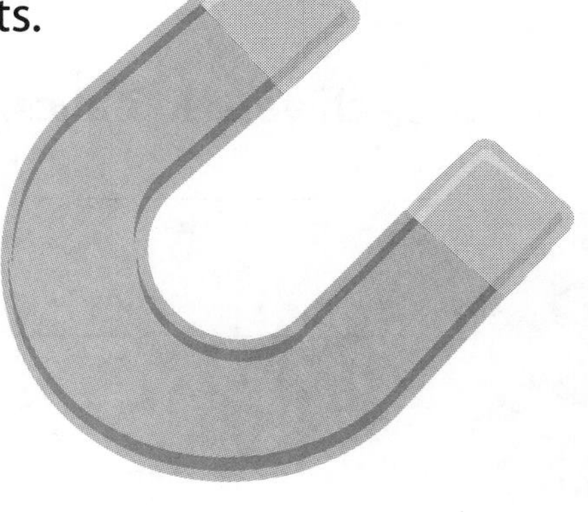

B Underline the main verb in each sentence.

1. Arturo has investigated energy.
2. He will learn that light is energy from the sun.
3. Batteries can store energy.
4. Some machines will convert stored energy to motion and heat.
5. Water and sound waves can carry energy from one place to another.

C Circle the helping verb that best completes each sentence.

1. Chen (will been) use a magnifying glass.
2. He (might am) look at a rock with it.
3. Scientists (can have) discovered that some rocks are harder than others.
4. They (is are) making a hypothesis.
5. Lee (will were) test limestone to see whether it cracks.

Name .... Date ....

43 Principal Parts of Verbs

A verb has four **principal parts.**

PRESENT	PRESENT PARTICIPLE	PAST	PAST PARTICIPLE
walk	**walking**	**walked**	**walked**

PRESENT PARTICIPLE: a verb that ends in *-ing* and is used with *am, is, are, was,* or *were*

Harold is unfolding the world map.

PAST: a verb that usually ends in *-d* or *-ed.* It is not used with a helping verb.

Liam learned the difference between maps and globes.

PAST PARTICIPLE: a verb that usually ends in *-d* or *-ed*, used with *has, have,* or *had.*

He has used the scale to measure distances.

For each verb in italics, write *present, past,* or *past participle* on the line.

_______________ 1. The twins have *measured* the distance on the map from New York City to Los Angeles.

_______________ 2. Once students *understand* the map scale, the distance is easy to figure out.

_______________ 3. Our visitors *used* a globe to point out the Amazon River in South America.

_______________ 4. Karim has *remembered* that the Himalaya Mountains are in northern India.

_______________ 5. He *locates* them by using the map legend.

_______________ 6. The compass has *helped* the class decide which way is north.

_______________ 7. Northern countries *include* Russia, Finland, and Canada.

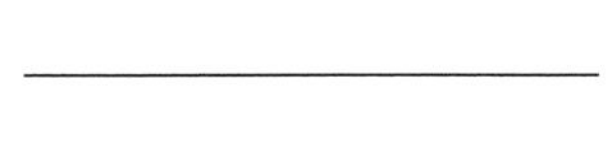

_______________ 8. The grid on the map *helped* us compare the sizes of countries.

_______________ 9. Each group has *traced* the map of a different state.

_______________ 10. The United States of America *is* in the Northern Hemisphere.

Verbs

Name .... Date ....

44 Regular Verbs and Irregular Verbs

The past and the past participle of **regular verbs** usually end in *-d* or *-ed*. The past and the past participle of **irregular verbs** are not formed by adding *-d* or *-ed* to the present. The past participle is always used with *has, have,* or *had.*

Clean is a regular verb.

PRESENT: **clean** PAST: **cleaned** PAST PARTICIPLE: **(has) cleaned**

Go is an irregular verb.

PRESENT: **go** PAST: **went** PAST PARTICIPLE: **(has) gone**

A Complete the chart of regular verbs.

PRESENT	PAST	PAST PARTICIPLE
1. wash	____________	(has) ____________
2. talk	____________	(has) ____________
3. review	____________	(has) ____________
4. yell	____________	(has) ____________
5. trick	____________	(has) ____________

B Complete the chart of irregular verbs.

PRESENT	PAST	PAST PARTICIPLE
1. give	____________	(have) ____________
2. see	____________	(have) ____________
3. sit	____________	(have) ____________
4. come	____________	(have) ____________
5. write	____________	(have) ____________

C Write whether each verb in italics is regular or irregular.

____________ 1. My brother has *fed* our dog every day this week.

____________ 2. I have *brushed* her.

____________ 3. We *take* the dog to the groomer, Mr. Charles, today.

____________ 4. Mr. Charles has *worked* in town for years.

____________ 5. He has *put* a bow on the dog's crate after each visit.

Verbs

Name .... Date ....

45 *Bring*

Bring is an irregular verb. The principal parts of *bring* are listed below.

PRESENT	PRESENT PARTICIPLE	PAST	PAST PARTICIPLE
bring	**bringing**	**brought**	**brought**

The present participle is used with a helping verb such as *am, is, are, was,* or *were.* The past participle is used with a helping verb such as *has, have,* or *had.*

A Complete each sentence with the correct form of *bring*.

1. ______________ up local problems with your city government.
2. The students ______________ the river pollution problem to the mayor.
3. Others have ______________ this same issue to the city council.
4. The mayor has ______________ in experts to talk about the need for clean rivers.
5. Some students are ______________ trash bags, rakes, and gloves to clean up the riverbank.

B Write a sentence about each topic, using the verb shown.

1. Topic: beach — Verb Form: bring

____

2. Topic: park — Verb Form: bringing

____

3. Topic: river — Verb Form: has brought

____

4. Topic: school — Verb Form: brought

____

5. Topic: citizens — Verb Form: have brought

____

Name .... Date ....

46 Buy

Buy is an irregular verb. The principal parts of *buy* are listed below.

PRESENT	PRESENT PARTICIPLE	PAST	PAST PARTICIPLE
buy	**buying**	**bought**	**bought**

The present participle is used with a helping verb such as *am, is, are, was,* or *were.* The past participle is used with a helping verb such as *has, have,* or *had.*

A Complete each sentence with the correct form of *buy.*

1. Will you __________ a book to donate to the library?
2. Last year my aunt __________ a book for the library in honor of my birthday.
3. The class has __________ many books for our library in the past.
4. I usually __________ a book I want to read.
5. Please __________ this book about China.
6. Last year Maureen __________ a book about Italy.
7. I am __________ that book for myself to keep.
8. If you __________ a book for the library, many people can read it.
9. I did not __________ a book for myself.
10. I __________ a book in order to help the library.

B For each verb in italics, write *present, present participle, past,* or *past participle* on the line.

__________________ 1. Some teachers have *bought* special materials for the classroom.

__________________ 2. Mr. Markin *bought* the best microscope I have ever seen for our class.

__________________ 3. My gym teacher already *bought* new basketballs.

__________________ 4. The art teachers *buy* paints for each student.

__________________ 5. Sara is *buying* a centimeter ruler for math class.

Name .... Date ....

47 Come

Come is an irregular verb. The principal parts of *come* are listed below.

PRESENT	PRESENT PARTICIPLE	PAST	PAST PARTICIPLE
come	**coming**	**came**	**come**

The present participle is used with a helping verb such as *am, is, are, was,* or *were*. The past participle is used with a helping verb such as *has, have,* or *had*.

A Complete each sentence with the correct form of *come*.

1. Today we have __________ to the library to research our state.
2. Our class __________ to research natural resources yesterday.
3. The librarian is __________ to tell about reference books.
4. Business leaders have __________ to talk about what makes our city and state great.
5. People originally __________ to our city because of the river and the railroad.
6. Tourists often __________ to our state to enjoy its natural beauty.
7. Of all the classes, ours has __________ to the library most often.
8. The governor of our state is __________ to visit our community.
9. She had __________ to visit once before.
10. The governor and the mayor __________ to our school to talk about transportation last year.

B Underline the verb that best completes each sentence.

1. Our county treasurer (come came) to talk about taxes.
2. The treasurer has (come came) to speak to the third grade.
3. Our class (come came) to the gym to hear him speak about government in this century.
4. The principal and the librarian have (come came) in the past.
5. Will a county judge (come came) to talk about laws?

Verbs

Name .... Date ....

48 *Sit*

Sit is an irregular verb. The principal parts of *sit* are listed below.

PRESENT	PRESENT PARTICIPLE	PAST	PAST PARTICIPLE
sit	**sitting**	**sat**	**sat**

The present participle is used with a helping verb such as *am, is, are, was,* or *were*. The past participle is used with a helping verb such as *has, have,* or *had*.

A Read the following paragraph. Underline the principal parts of *sit*.

We sat in the front row at the circus yesterday. A woman in a sparkly dress was sitting on an elephant's back. A trapeze artist sat on a swing high above the crowd. An animal trainer told a lion, "Sit down, please." The lion sat quietly on a rug.

B Complete each sentence with the correct form of *sit*.

1. Michaela ______________ on a plane when she flew to Washington, D.C.
2. Her parents were ______________ next to her.
3. Tourists often ______________ in the Capitol to watch laws being made.
4. They are ______________ in the balcony seats called the gallery.
5. The vice president ______________ down after he spoke.
6. After a long day, the family ______________ by the hotel pool.
7. Several rocking chairs are ______________ around the pool.
8. Michaela's mother told her that President Kennedy had ______________ in a rocking chair to rest his back.
9. President Roosevelt ______________ in a wheelchair for part of his life.
10. At the Roosevelt Memorial, a statue of the president's dog ______________ next to the president's statue.

Verbs

Name .... Date ....

49 *Eat*

Eat is an irregular verb. The principal parts of *eat* are listed below.

PRESENT	PRESENT PARTICIPLE	PAST	PAST PARTICIPLE
eat	**eating**	**ate**	**eaten**

The present participle is used with a helping verb such as *am, is, are, was,* or *were.* The past participle is used with a helping verb such as *has, have,* or *had*.

A **Complete each sentence with the correct form of *eat*.**

1. Good nutrition means that each day people __________ healthful meals.
2. Yesterday Hailey __________ rice cakes for a snack.
3. Jee has __________ a hot lunch in the cafeteria every day this year.
4. For good health __________ an apple instead of candy as a snack.
5. Have you __________ a nutritious lunch?
6. Most children like to __________ cake at birthday parties.
7. Everyone should try to __________ fruits and vegetables each day.
8. You can get sick if you have __________ too much food that is not nutritious.
9. Marty was __________ a bunch of grapes.
10. Ms. Flores has __________ green vegetables almost every day of her life.

B **Replace the word in italics with *eat, eating, ate,* or *eaten*.**

__________ 1. Humberto and Luz *bring* tortillas.

__________ 2. They have *chosen* mild jalapeño peppers.

__________ 3. Luz is *cooking* only a small portion of corn.

__________ 4. Papa has *enjoyed* all the tostadas.

__________ 5. Tía Alba *prepared* the spicy bean soup.

Name .... Date ....

50 *Go*

Go is an irregular verb. The principal parts of *go* are listed below.

PRESENT	PRESENT PARTICIPLE	PAST	PAST PARTICIPLE
go	**going**	**went**	**gone**

The present participle is used with a helping verb such as *am, is, are, was,* or *were.* The past participle is used with a helping verb such as *has, have,* or *had.*

A Choose the correct form of *go* for each sentence.

1. Please __________ to the straw mat, a Kwanzaa symbol of tradition.
2. I am __________ to my uncle's house for this African American holiday.
3. Mother has __________ to get the seven candles.
4. She __________ to the front of the room to tell what each candle means.
5. We __________ to the table each of the seven nights to light one of the candles.

B Circle the correct form of *go* to complete each sentence.

1. My family and I always (go went gone) to Kwanzaa celebrations.
2. We have (go went gone) to a feast every year that I can remember.
3. We (go went gone) every December 31.
4. Kiandra has (go went gone) with her family.
5. She (go went gone) to celebrate her family's history.
6. Does your family (go going gone) to any special festivals?
7. Each year we have (go going gone) to the ceremony as a family.
8. My best friend is (go going gone) with us this year.
9. I (go went gone) to my first celebration when I was a baby.
10. Are you (go going gone) too?

Name .... Date ....

51 *See*

See is an irregular verb. The principal parts of *see* are listed below.

PRESENT	PRESENT PARTICIPLE	PAST	PAST PARTICIPLE
see	**seeing**	**saw**	**seen**

The present participle is used with a helping verb such as *am, is, are, was,* or *were*. The past participle is used with a helping verb such as *has, have,* or *had*.

A **Read the following paragraph about California. Underline the principal parts of *see.***

Residents and tourists have seen the beauty of California. They can see oceans, coastlines, mountains, and valleys. Last year when I visited, I saw the desert. I have seen all these features on a physical map. My class sees the Sacramento River on the map.

B **Circle the correct form of *see* in each sentence.**

1. Early explorers (see saw seen) great wonders in California.
2. Unfortunately, not many of them (see saw seen) gold.
3. Many people have (see saw seen) the pretty mountains.
4. My grandfather has (see seeing seen) new industry begin in California.
5. Mother is (see seeing seen) all her family in Sacramento.

C **Write the correct form of *see* on each line.**

1. You can __________ symbols in a medicine wheel.
2. Did you __________ the circle that represents the Circle of Life?
3. You have __________ the wooden totem poles.
4. This morning Nadia __________ an eagle.
5. She always feels peaceful after she has __________ an eagle.

Name .... Date ....

52 *Take*

Take is an irregular verb. The principal parts of *take* are listed below.

PRESENT	PRESENT PARTICIPLE	PAST	PAST PARTICIPLE
take	**taking**	**took**	**taken**

The present participle is used with a helping verb such as *am, is, are, was,* or *were.* The past participle is used with a helping verb such as *has, have,* or *had.*

A Complete each sentence with the correct form of *take.*

1. Ruth is____________ a tour of memorials in Washington, D.C.
2. Her guide has ____________ time to explain the meaning of each memorial.
3. She ____________ a trip into history at every monument or building.
4. The bus tour of the memorials ____________ two hours.
5. Yesterday some people ____________ a walking tour of the memorials.
6. Justin ____________ a picture of the Lincoln Memorial.
7. Martin Luther King Jr. has ____________ a place among American heroes.
8. Martin Luther King Jr. ____________ civil rights seriously.
9. King spoke out against those who were ____________ away the rights of African Americans.
10. Americans have____________ care to remember his work.

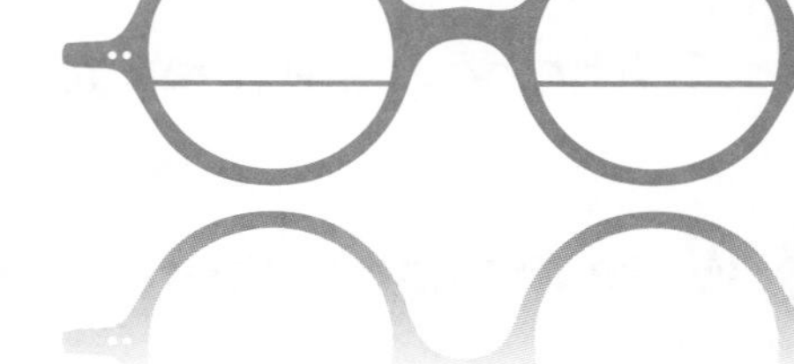

B Write *PR* for present, *P* for past, or *PP* for past participle over the forms of *take.*

"Benjamin Franklin took care of people's needs with some of his inventions," my father says as he takes off his glasses. "Franklin made bifocals popular, but some of the work he took part in protects us. You know that he had taken an interest in electricity. Did you know that he invented lightning rods to protect buildings from fire? He also started the first fire brigade. Let's take a few minutes to research his other ideas."

Verbs

Name .... Date ....

53 *Tear*

Tear is an irregular verb. The principal parts of *tear* are listed below.

PRESENT	PRESENT PARTICIPLE	PAST	PAST PARTICIPLE
tear	**tearing**	**tore**	**torn**

The present participle is used with a helping verb such as *am, is, are, was,* or *were.* The past participle is used with a helping verb such as *has, have,* or *had.*

A Underline the form of ***tear*** in each sentence.

1. The students in Mr. Ito's class are tearing paper for their art projects.
2. Beth carefully tore thin red paper to make a flower.
3. She has also torn green paper to make leaves.
4. She was tearing paper for the stem when the bell rang.
5. She will tear the rest of the paper tomorrow.

B Circle the correct form of ***tear*** for each sentence.

1. Those boys are (tear tearing) paper to make lion masks.
2. George has (torn tore) a sheet of construction paper into a round shape.
3. He (tore tear) holes in the paper for eyes.
4. Now he is (tearing tore) pieces for the mane.
5. The boys are (tear tearing) their paper very carefully.

C Write the correct form of ***tear*** on the line.

1. Ana and Sue are ______________ magazine pages to make collages.
2. They have ______________ different shapes and sizes.
3. You can ______________ the paper into any shapes you like.
4. Earlier, Ana ______________ heavy paper to make a frame.
5. Mr. Ito is ______________ gold paper to make stars.

Verbs

Name .... Date ....

54 *Write*

Write is an irregular verb. The principal parts of *write* are listed below.

PRESENT	PRESENT PARTICIPLE	PAST	PAST PARTICIPLE
write	**writing**	**wrote**	**written**

The present participle is used with a helping verb such as *am, is, are, was,* or *were.* The past participle is used with a helping verb such as *has, have,* or *had.*

A Complete each sentence with the correct form of *write*.

1. Who ______________ the Declaration of Independence?
2. Thomas Jefferson had ______________ the first draft 20 years before he became president.
3. Americans ______________ the U.S. Constitution to name the basic laws of their new country.
4. Abbey has______________ a report about the U.S. Constitution.
5. Senators ______________ laws for everyone in the country.
6. Members of Congress ______________ laws that are later debated at the U.S. Capitol.
7. Some senators are ______________ laws about education.
8. Our U.S. representative ______________ a law to help the elderly.
9. What laws would you have ______________ ?
10. I ______________ letters to the members of Congress from my state.

B Put a check mark before each statement that is written correctly.

______ 1. Students have written about the Statue of Liberty.

______ 2. They written how it is a great symbol of freedom.

______ 3. Who wrote about other symbols?

______ 4. Oscar has written about the bald eagle.

______ 5. Ben and Troy have wrote a poem about the flag.

Verbs

Name .... Date ....

55 Irregular Verbs

A **Complete the chart of irregular verbs.**

PRESENT	PAST	PAST PARTICIPLE
1. bring	______	(has) ______
2. run	______	(has) ______
3. eat	______	(has) ______
4. go	______	(has) ______
5. sit	______	(has) ______

B **Complete the chart of irregular verbs.**

PAST	PRESENT	PRESENT PARTICIPLE
1. saw	______	(is) ______
2. bought	______	(is) ______
3. came	______	(is) ______
4. took	______	(is) ______
5. wrote	______	(is) ______

C **Write a sentence for each verb.**

1. give

______

2. am giving

______

3. gave

______

4. has given

______

5. were giving

______

Name .... Date ....

56 Simple Present Tense

The tense of a verb shows when the action takes place. A verb in the **simple present tense** tells about something that is always true or about an action that happens again and again.

A planet orbits the sun.

Telescopes magnify the stars.

A Circle the correct verb in each sentence.

1. Earth (move moves) around the sun.
2. The sun (provide provides) heat and energy.
3. The moon (reflect reflects) light from the sun.
4. Some stars (appear appears) to shine brighter during different seasons.
5. Satellites (take takes) pictures from space.
6. Scientists (study studies) the images.
7. Cartographers (use uses) the images to improve maps.
8. Astronauts (explore explores) space.
9. Mars (seem seems) to have no life.
10. An observatory (contain contains) a large, powerful telescope.

B Match each subject noun with a verb. Match nouns 1 through 5 with verbs a through e. Match nouns 6 through 10 with verbs f through j.

	NOUN	VERB		NOUN	VERB
______	1. astronauts	a. spins	______	6. telescopes	f. flies
______	2. stars	b. shine	______	7. the shuttle	g. experiment
______	3. Earth	c. spacewalk	______	8. sunlight	h. magnify
______	4. satellites	d. shoots	______	9. a planet	i. heats
______	5. a comet	e. orbit	______	10. researchers	j. rotates

Verbs

Name .... Date ....

57 Simple Past Tense

A verb in the **simple past tense** tells about something that happened in the past.

John looked at stories, myths, and legends as ways to understand human beings.

A Circle the verb that shows past tense.

1. Robinson Crusoe (land landed) on a deserted island.
2. He (see saw) that he had to provide for himself.
3. John (knows knew) that he could learn about survival from reading about Crusoe.
4. Tall tales (showed show) the American spirit.
5. Characters such as Paul Bunyan and Pecos Bill (stand stood) larger than life.
6. Myths and legends often (told tell) about imaginary characters with great accomplishments or ideas.
7. Stories about some real people, such as Daniel Boone and Davy Crockett, (become became) legends.
8. In Greek myths Zeus (rule ruled) the gods.
9. In the legend of King Arthur, the knights (sit sat) at a round table.
10. Native Americans (use used) stories about the past to teach children about their beliefs.

B Write the past tense of each verb.

PRESENT	PAST	PRESENT	PAST
1. go	____________	6. jump	____________
2. take	____________	7. throw	____________
3. eat	____________	8. remember	____________
4. learn	____________	9. come	____________
5. buy	____________	10. read	____________

Verbs

Name .... Date ....

58 Future Tense with *Will*

The word *will* is one way to express something that will take place in the future. The helping verb *will* is used with the present part of a verb to form a future tense.

I will send the invitations to our parents.

A Circle the words in each sentence that show the future tense.

1. Mrs. Gonzales will help you with your science project.
2. Katy will show you where the supplies are.
3. Tim will read the directions aloud.
4. Gloria will hold the frame in place.
5. You will be happy with the results.
6. We will have our science fair on Saturday.
7. Mrs. Gonzales will help us get ready.
8. Tom and Joe will put the tables in the gym.
9. Karen and Katy will make posters.
10. Ryan will hang the posters in the hall.

B Rewrite each sentence in the future tense, using *will.*

1. The students prepare their experiments.

___

2. Our parents arrive at two o'clock.

___

3. Jacob takes the tickets.

___

4. Mrs. Gonzales greets the audience.

___

5. The judges vote for the best project.

___

Name .... Date ....

59 Future Tense with *Going to*

Like *will,* the phrase *going to* is used to express something that will happen in the future. A form of the helping verb *be* (*am, is, are, was,* or *were*) must be used in front of *going to. Going to* is followed by the present part of the verb.

What are you going to do on your vacation?

I am going to visit my cousin in Boston.

A Underline the future tense phrase and verb in each sentence.

1. We are going to walk the Freedom Trail.
2. We are going to follow the footsteps painted on the sidewalk.
3. I am going to visit the Old North Church.
4. My cousin is going to show me Paul Revere's house.
5. I am going to see a statue of Benjamin Franklin.
6. We are going to watch the ducks in the Boston Public Garden.
7. I am going to ride on a Swan Boat there.
8. My parents are going to see the John F. Kennedy Library.
9. My dad is going to drive across the Bunker Hill Bridge.
10. My cousin is going to take me to the New England Aquarium.

B Rewrite each sentence in the future tense, using *going to.*

1. We watched the baby penguins there.

   ____

2. I climbed the rock wall in the Boston Children's Museum.

   ____

3. My cousin and I attended a Red Sox game.

   ____

4. My mom bought souvenirs in Faneuil Hall.

   ____

5. We had a great time!

   ____

Verbs

Name .... Date ....

60 Present Progressive Tense

A verb in the **present progressive tense** tells what is happening now. This tense is formed with *am, is,* or *are* and the present participle.

Our class is visiting the zoo today.

Put a check in front of each sentence that uses a verb in the present progressive tense. Circle all the verbs in the present progressive tense.

_____ 1. We are staying at the zoo all day.

_____ 2. The penguin house at the zoo is attracting the most visitors.

_____ 3. The children watched the penguins eat.

_____ 4. The penguins are eating small fish.

_____ 5. A line of four penguins waddled across the ice.

_____ 6. The penguins are standing with their backs to the visitors.

_____ 7. One penguin is sleeping with its bill tucked under a flipper.

_____ 8. Another penguin is building a nest with stones.

_____ 9. The temperature was 30 degrees Fahrenheit in the penguin house.

_____ 10. Our teacher took a class picture in front of the exhibit.

_____ 11. I am buying postcards of the penguins.

_____ 12. We enjoyed our trip to the zoo.

_____ 13. The zookeeper is traveling to Antarctica to study emperor penguins.

_____ 14. Some kinds of penguins are living near the equator.

_____ 15. Our class is doing an art project about penguins.

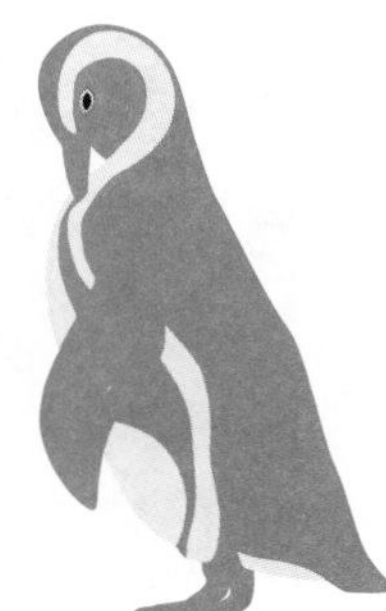

Name .... Date ....

61 Past Progressive Tense

A verb in the **past progressive tense** tells what was happening in the past. This tense is formed with *was* or *were* and the present participle.

Our whole family was walking through the forest.

Put a check in front of each sentence that uses a verb in the past progressive tense. Circle all the verbs in the past progressive tense.

_____ 1. The boys were watching the baseball game on television.

_____ 2. Maureen was shooting free throws at basketball practice.

_____ 3. My brothers were playing hockey.

_____ 4. James Naismith invented basketball in 1891.

_____ 5. Mom was jogging when the sun came up.

_____ 6. She was listening to music while she ran.

_____ 7. Greg was building a jigsaw puzzle after school.

_____ 8. Marbles and bowling are examples of target games.

_____ 9. Dad was going to the golf course when the rain started.

_____ 10. Their coach was calling for a time-out.

_____ 11. My aunt and uncle were meeting us at the soccer match.

_____ 12. Board games use pieces moved on a flat surface.

_____ 13. The children were performing a play in the backyard.

_____ 14. Marcie was using dominoes to practice addition.

_____ 15. Our class played card games to practice multiplication facts.

Name .... Date ....

62 *Is* and *Are*, *Was* and *Were*

Is, are, was, and *were* are being verbs. These words do not express action.
Use *is* or *was* with a singular subject.

Pottery is one kind of art.

Picasso was a modern painter.

Use *are* or *were* with a plural subject.

Sculptors are famous for perfecting shape.

The Impressionists were painters.

PAINT

A Complete each sentence with *is* or *are*.

1. The photographs by Ansel Adams __________ in black and white.
2. John James Audubon __________ a world-renowned painter of birds.
3. Mobiles __________ among Alexander Calder's greatest achievements.
4. A flower __________ beautiful to Georgia O'Keeffe.
5. Mothers and babies __________ subjects of Mary Cassatt's paintings.
6. Paul Cézanne __________ often called the father of modern art.
7. Grandma Moses __________ famous for her paintings of country life.
8. Faith Ringgold's quilts __________ works of art.
9. Many drawings by M. C. Escher __________ examples of images with no beginning or end.
10. Jacob Lawrence's portraits of black leaders __________ bold and lifelike.

B Read the paragraph. Complete each sentence with *was* or *were*.

Leonardo da Vinci __________ a great artist, inventor, and engineer. He __________ known for painting the *Mona Lisa*, a picture of a woman. Flying machines and the flight of birds __________ part of his studies. One of his inventions __________ an underwater diving suit. In Leonardo's lifetime many of his inventions __________ only on paper.

Verbs

Name .... Date ....

63 Contractions with *Not*

A **contraction** is a short way to write some words. An apostrophe (') marks the place where one or more letters have been left out of a word.

The word *not* is often part of a contraction. The letter *o* is left out, and an apostrophe is used in its place. Here are some contractions with *not.*

aren't = are not	**don't = do not**
wasn't = was not	**didn't = did not**
can't = cannot	**won't = will not**

A **Draw a line to match the words in Column A to the contractions in Column B.**

	COLUMN A	COLUMN B		COLUMN A	COLUMN B
1.	were not	isn't	6.	does not	won't
2.	is not	didn't	7.	are not	hadn't
3.	cannot	weren't	8.	was not	doesn't
4.	do not	can't	9.	will not	aren't
5.	did not	don't	10.	had not	wasn't

B **Complete each sentence with the contraction for the words on the left.**

cannot	1. I ____________ remember what a line of longitude is.
does not	2. ____________ a line of longitude pass through the North Pole and the South Pole on a globe?
was not	3. I ____________ able to find the equator by looking at the center of the globe.
will not	4. When you travel from New York to London, you ____________ cross the equator.
are not	5. Canada and Europe ____________ in the Southern Hemisphere.

Verbs

Name.. Date......................

64 Reviewing Verbs

A **On the line write *A* for action verb or *B* for being verb to identify the verb in italics in each sentence.**

______ 1. Animals *are* an important part of the circle of life.

______ 2. Some reptiles *survive* in and out of water.

______ 3. A cow *is* a mammal.

______ 4. Some fish *are* able to jump out of the water.

______ 5. Birds *build* nests in many ways.

B **Circle the correct verb for each sentence.
Write *present* or *past* on the line.**

____________ 6. Mary Azarian (win won) a Caldecott Medal for her illustrations in the book *Snowflake Bentley*.

____________ 7. *Salmon Summer* by Bruce McMillan (tells told) the story of a boy fishing in Alaska.

____________ 8. Yesterday we (talked talks) about the book *Martha Calling* by Susan Meddaugh.

____________ 9. The Newbery Medal winner (wrote write) the best children's book last year.

____________ 10. Every year Caldecott Medal winners (create created) the finest illustrations in children's books.

C **Write the past and the past participle of each verb.**

PRESENT	PAST	PAST PARTICIPLE
11. buy	____________	(had) ____________
12. write	____________	(had) ____________
13. sit	____________	(had) ____________
14. take	____________	(had) ____________
15. see	____________	(had) ____________

eat S w coat i r eye t big r

Verbs

Continued →

Name .... Date ....

D **Circle the helping verb and underline the main verb in each sentence.**

16. Justin is reading a timeline of air travel.
17. Ann and Mary are looking for the year of the first supersonic flight.
18. The class has found the flight of Orville and Wilbur Wright in 1903.
19. The first manned mission to the moon was flown in 1969.
20. Before the Mars rover landed, the first space shuttle had rocketed to fame in 1981.

E **Circle the verb in each sentence. On the line write *R* if the verb is regular or *I* if it is irregular.**

_____ 21. Egyptians built the Great Pyramids.

_____ 22. The Maya constructed stone temples in Mexico and Central America.

_____ 23. The Chinese people felt safe behind the Great Wall of China.

_____ 24. The statue of Zeus at Olympia honored a Greek god.

_____ 25. Native American children learned to respect the land.

Try It Yourself

Write three sentences about a place you have visited. Use at least one verb that shows action, one that is in the past tense, and one that is irregular.

____

____

____

Check Your Own Work

Choose a piece of writing from your writing portfolio, a work in progress, an assignment from another class, or a letter. Revise it, using the skills you have reviewed. This checklist will help you.

✔ Have you used a helping verb when needed?

✔ Have you spelled past tense verbs correctly, including irregular verbs?

✔ Have you used the past participle with *has, had,* or *have*?

Name .... Date ....

65 Adjectives

Adjectives describe nouns. They can tell how something looks, tastes, sounds, feels, or smells. In this sentence the nouns are underlined, and the adjectives are in italics.

***Many* children have a *favorite* author.**

A Circle the adjective that describes the underlined noun.

1. Beverly Cleary is a famous author.
2. She writes enjoyable stories about children and their families.
3. Boys and girls enjoy the funny tales of Ramona Quimby.
4. Ramona is a delightful character.
5. My favorite book is *Ramona and Her Father.*
6. Beverly Cleary won a special award for that book.
7. Ramona once crowned herself with prickly burrs.
8. Her father worked hard to comb her messy hair.
9. What splendid pictures Ramona and her father drew.
10. They shared happy days together.

B Complete each sentence with an adjective that describes the noun in italics.

1. Jill walked into the ____________________ *library*.
2. She opened the ____________________ *door* and went inside.
3. A ____________________ *librarian* helped her.
4. She directed Jill to a ____________________ *room*.
5. ____________________ *children* were in the room.
6. Some students looked at ____________________ *books*.
7. Jill hoped to find a ____________________ *book*.
8. Others listened to ____________________ *stories* on tape.
9. Jill walked over to the ____________________ *exhibit*.
10. She liked the ____________________ *pictures* best.

Name .... Date ....

66 Adjectives Before Nouns

Most adjectives describe size, shape, color, weight, age, or other features of nouns. They are called **descriptive adjectives.** Descriptive adjectives usually come before the nouns they describe.

The tall man was carrying a heavy bag.

In the example above, *tall* describes *man,* and *heavy* describes *bag.*

A **Underline the descriptive adjective in each sentence. Circle the noun that it describes.**

1. Flamingos are beautiful birds.
2. They have pink feathers.
3. Flamingos often live in muddy lagoons.
4. They wade though the water on long legs.
5. Flamingos eat seeds, plants, and small animals such as crawfish.
6. They filter food from the water through their large beaks.
7. Flamingos live in huge flocks.
8. They are found in places with tropical weather.
9. Flamingos need fresh water to drink.
10. Some of them drink hot water from geysers.

B **Complete each sentence with a descriptive adjective. Underline the noun that each adjective describes.**

1. Mom and I made a ____________________ salad for dinner.
2. I shredded some ____________________ lettuce.
3. Mom sliced some ____________________ carrots.
4. We added some ____________________ beets.
5. I sprinkled on some ____________________ cheese.

Name .... Date ....

67 Subject Complements

Some descriptive adjectives come after being verbs such as *am, is, are, was,* and *were.* Those adjectives are called **subject complements.** A subject complement tells more about the subject of a sentence. In this sentence the subject is underlined and the subject complements are in italics.

The hike is *long* and *difficult.*

A **Circle the subject complement or subject complements in each sentence. Each subject is underlined.**

1. The trail was hilly and rocky.
2. The trees in the forest are tall.
3. The bridge was large and dark.
4. The squirrels in the tree are noisy.
5. The butterflies were graceful and colorful.
6. The songs of the birds were cheerful.
7. A cloud was white and fluffy.
8. The rain was cold.
9. The trail is slippery in the rain.
10. The hikers were tired after their walk.

B **Complete each sentence with an adjective from the list. Use each adjective once.**

1. The mountains are ________________ .
2. The water in mountain streams is ________________ .
3. Hiking in the mountains is ________________ .
4. The weather at the coast is ________________ .
5. The climbers were ________________ .

Name .... Date ....

68 Compound Subject Complements

Some sentences have more than one subject complement. Two adjectives joined by *and, but,* or *or* after a being verb form a **compound subject complement.** Both adjectives tell more about the subject.

The popcorn was crunchy and salty.

A Underline the subject complements in each sentence. Circle the noun or pronoun they describe.

1. The party was fun and festive.
2. The decorations were bright and colorful.
3. Their hamburgers were juicy and tasty.
4. My cider was spicy and warm.
5. The corn was hot and buttery.
6. Some games were silly or tricky.
7. The costumes were funny or scary.
8. Prizes were popular and inexpensive.
9. The band was small but loud.
10. By evening I was tired and happy.

B Complete each sentence with a compound subject complement. Choose from these adjectives.

brown	flexible	gray	Asian	sharp
curved	African	heavy	long	tall

1. Elephants are ____________ and ____________.
2. The two kinds of elephants are ____________ and ____________.
3. Their tusks are ____________ and ____________.
4. An elephant's trunk is ____________ and ____________.
5. Elephants are usually ____________ or ____________.

Adjectives

Name .... Date ....

69 Adjectives That Compare

Many adjectives that compare two nouns end with *-er*.

The Mississippi River is longer than the Minnesota River.

Many adjectives that compare three or more nouns end with *-est*.

The longest river in the world is the Nile River in Africa.

A Circle the correct adjective in parentheses.

1. The (deeper deepest) lake in the world is in Siberia.
2. The Caspian Sea is (larger largest) than Lake Superior.
3. Lake Michigan is (warmer warmest) than Lake Superior.
4. Lake Erie is (smaller smallest) than Lake Michigan.
5. Lake Ontario is the (smaller smallest) lake of the five Great Lakes.

B Complete each pair of sentences, using the given words.

taller tallest

1. Which is the ______________ mountain in the United States?
2. This mountain is ______________ than that one.

steeper steepest

3. The trail up the mountain was ______________ than he thought.
4. This section of trail is the ______________ part so far.

colder coldest

5. At what time of day is the temperature ______________ ?
6. I was ______________ in the morning than in the afternoon.

higher highest

7. That goat has climbed ______________ than we have.
8. Of all the mountain peaks, that one is the ______________ peak.

harder hardest

9. The ______________ part of the hike was the climb.
10. Climbing down was ______________ than I thought it would be.

Name .... Date ....

70 More Adjectives That Compare

Adjectives that compare often end in *-er* or *-est.* Here are some spelling rules for making adjectives that compare.

If an adjective ends in *e,* drop the final *e* and add *-er* or *-est.*

wide **wider** **widest**

If an adjective ends in *y* following a consonant, change the *y* to *i* and add *-er* or *-est.*

happy **happier** **happiest**

If an adjective ends in a consonant that follows a vowel double the final consonant before adding *-er* or *-est.*

hot **hotter** **hottest**

A **Write the correct words in the chart.**

ADJECTIVE	COMPARE TWO NOUNS	COMPARE MORE THAN TWO NOUNS
1. chilly	______________	______________
2. flat	______________	______________
3. safe	______________	______________
4. big	______________	______________
5. tricky	______________	______________
6. pale	______________	______________
7. sad	______________	______________
8. tiny	______________	______________
9. large	______________	______________
10. snowy	______________	______________

B **Underline the adjective that compares in each sentence.**

1. Mexico City is the largest city in North America.
2. Mexico City is bigger than New York City.
3. Boston is windier than Chicago.
4. The weather is much hotter in Tampa than in Seattle.
5. San Diego may have the nicest weather in the United States.

Name .... Date ....

71 Irregular Adjectives That Compare

Some adjectives that compare are irregular. They are not formed by adding *-er* or *-est*. Two common irregular adjectives are *good* and *bad.*

	COMPARE TWO NOUNS	COMPARE THREE OR MORE NOUNS
good	**better**	**best**
bad	**worse**	**worst**

A Write *good, better,* or *best* to complete each sentence.

1. Yesterday our team played its ____________ game ever.
2. Our offense was ____________ than theirs.
3. We made some really ____________ plays.
4. The defense was ____________ in the second half than in the first half.
5. Hank made the ____________ play of the game.

B Write *bad, worse,* or *worst* to complete each sentence.

1. Last night the weather reporter said, "There is no ____________ weather, only bad clothes."
2. She has not been to Mount Washington, which has some of the ____________ weather anywhere.
3. Mount Washington is in New Hampshire, but its weather can be as ____________ as Antarctica's.
4. The wind and snow are ____________ there than at most places.
5. Areas that are in mountains often have the ____________ winter temperatures in the United States.

C Complete each sentence to make it true about you.

1. My best subject is ________________________________.
2. I am better at ________________ than ________________.
3. I am worst at playing ________________________________.
4. I am good at making ________________________________.
5. My best friend is ________________________________.

Adjectives

Name .... Date ....

72 Adjectives That Tell How Many

Some adjectives tell exactly how many: *first, six, eight, thirty*.

Joel has twelve math problems left to do.

Some adjectives tell about how many: *few, several, some*.

A few days ago we didn't have homework!

A Circle the adjective that tells how many. Write *E* if the adjective tells exactly how many. Write *A* if the adjective tells about how many.

_____ 1. Our class decided to earn some money for our school.

_____ 2. We decided to make fifty bookmarks.

_____ 3. Supplies to make each bookmark cost a few cents.

_____ 4. We sold each bookmark for twenty cents.

_____ 5. Our profit was several times what we earned last year.

B Underline the adjective that tells how many.

1. There were many stores in town.
2. Only three stores sold clothing.
3. Lisa needed a few new sweaters.
4. Tony wanted two pairs of shoes.
5. For several days they visited those clothing stores.
6. Lisa and Tony found things they wanted in each store.
7. Tony's shoes cost twenty dollars.
8. Lisa wished the sweaters cost less money.
9. Lisa realized she could not buy many sweaters with her savings.
10. Tony had only thirty-five cents left after he had paid for his shoes.

Adjectives

Name .... Date ....

73 Articles

A, an, and *the* point out nouns. They are called **articles.** *A* and *an* point out any one of a group of people, places, or things. Use *a* before a word that begins with a consonant sound. Use *an* before a word that begins with a vowel sound.

I heard a bluebird. I saw an eagle.

The points out a specific person, place, or thing.

The bluebird was on the branch.

I photographed the eagle as it flew by.

Circle the article in each sentence. Underline the noun that each article points out.

1. John James Audubon was a naturalist.
2. He was also an artist who painted pictures of birds.
3. The pictures that he painted are very famous.
4. Audubon was born on the island that is now called Haiti.
5. When he was 18, he moved to the commonwealth of Pennsylvania.
6. He went into business and drew pictures of birds as a hobby.
7. Later he worked full-time as a painter.
8. Audubon wanted to paint a picture of every kind of bird.
9. To do that, he studied the birds in their habitats.
10. Each of his paintings is a life-sized portrait of one kind of bird.

Audubon painted birds in their natural surroundings. He helped people appreciate wildlife. Give an example of how you might show respect for wildlife. Circle any articles in your writing.

Name .... Date ....

74 Demonstrative Adjectives

This, that, these, and *those* are **demonstrative adjectives.** They point out specific people, places, or things. *This* and *these* point to nouns that are near.

This pond feels warm.

That and *those* point to nouns that are farther away.

That swamp 20 miles away is an important ecosystem.

A Put an *X* on the line before the correct answer.

1. Which river is farther away?

   ______ This river is deep. ______ That river has a bridge.

2. Which lake is closer?

   ______ That lake is deep. ______ This lake is beautiful.

3. Which stream is farther away?

   ______ That stream dried up. ______ This stream is clean.

4. Which birds are closer?

   ______ These birds live here. ______ Those birds live there.

5. Which mountains are farther away?

   ______ These mountains are tall. ______ Those mountains are tall.

B Complete each sentence with *this* or *that,* according to the clues given.

1. __________ desert we are traveling through is hot.
2. Cactus grows in __________ desert but not here.
3. Toucans live in __________ rain forest, which is far away.
4. __________ forest we saw in the picture yesterday is in South America.
5. Look in __________ grassland area for any animals that might be here.

Adjectives

Name .... Date ....

75 Proper Adjectives

A **proper adjective** is formed from a proper noun. A proper adjective always begins with a capital letter.

PROPER NOUN	**Have you ever been to Mexico?**
PROPER ADJECTIVE	**I like Mexican food.**

Here are some examples of proper nouns and their proper adjectives.

NOUN	ADJECTIVE	NOUN	ADJECTIVE
China	**Chinese**	**Kenya**	**Kenyan**
Japan	**Japanese**	**Russia**	**Russian**
India	**Indian**	**France**	**French**
Poland	**Polish**	**Greece**	**Greek**

A **Underline the proper adjective in each sentence. Circle the noun it describes.**

1. My aunt bought me a warm Irish sweater.
2. This cuckoo clock came from a German store.
3. I made a sandwich with ham and Swiss cheese.
4. This Brazilian music is fun to dance to.
5. An African elephant has really large ears.

B **Complete each sentence with the proper adjective for the proper noun in parentheses. Use a dictionary if you need help.**

1. Spaghetti is my favorite ________________ food. (Italy)
2. Many people cross the ________________ border every day. (Canada)
3. Hans Christian Andersen was a ________________ writer. (Denmark)
4. The museum had a collection of ________________ art. (Vietnam)
5. My mom enjoys ________________ coffee. (Turkey)

Adjectives

Name .... Date ....

76 Nouns Used as Adjectives

Sometimes a noun can be used as an adjective. When two nouns are used together, the first one often acts as an adjective. It tells more about the second noun.

We bought apples at the fruit stand.

We made apple pie.

Circle each noun that is used as an adjective. Underline the noun it describes.

1. In the 1800s pioneers traveled to the West in simple farm wagons.
2. The wagons were fitted with canvas tops.
3. They were filled with food, tools, clothing, furniture, and household supplies.
4. Pioneer families had to fit all their belongings in the wagons.
5. Every day the pioneers ate a sunrise breakfast of bread and bacon before they hit the trail.
6. After walking for hours, they would have a lunch break, and then they would start walking again.
7. Around 6 p.m., the settlers would put their wagons in a circle to make a livestock corral.
8. After an evening meal, everyone went to sleep.
9. By the end of the long journey, the families had worn out their shoe leather.
10. Many pioneers built themselves log cabins when the journey was over.

Name .... Date ....

77 Reviewing Adjectives

A **Circle the adjective that describes each underlined noun.**

1. Graceful eagles soared through the air.
2. Once Mali saw playful lions through his binoculars.
3. The orange birds have short bills.
4. Children enjoy watching garden snakes.
5. We think donkeys are stubborn.

B **Decide whether the adjective in italics tells exactly how many or about how many. Write *exactly* or *about* on the line.**

_______________ 6. Kiyoshi traveled *many* miles to reach Asia.

_______________ 7. He visited the Great Wall of China on the *second* day of his trip.

_______________ 8. Arina knew that *numerous* islands make up the Philippines.

_______________ 9. She relaxed on an island beach for a *few* days.

_______________ 10. Jeb saw *six* elephants carry logs to a river in Thailand.

C **Choose the correct article for each noun. Write *a* or *an* on the line.**

_____ 11. mountain

_____ 12. island

_____ 13. volcano

_____ 14. river

_____ 15. inlet

_____ 16. peninsula

_____ 17. wetland

_____ 18. acre

_____ 19. earthquake

_____ 20. ocean

Adjectives

Continued →

Name .... Date ....

D **Circle the correct form of the word to compare the nouns in each sentence.**

21. January is (longer longest) than February.
22. The (colder coldest) temperatures in the world are in Antarctica.
23. The (brighter brightest) day of this year was during the summer.
24. Leaves are (prettier prettiest) in fall than in summer.
25. Seasons are (shorter shortest) than years.
26. A butterfly is (quicker quickest) than a caterpillar.
27. Caterpillars are some of the (slower slowest) animals in the world.
28. A caterpillar is (thinner thinnest) than its cocoon.
29. The (smaller smallest) butterfly has a wingspan of less than one centimeter.
30. The change from caterpillar to butterfly is (grander grandest) than anything else!

Try It Yourself

Close your eyes and imagine that you are in a desert, rain forest, or grassland. Write three sentences about this place, using adjectives to describe and compare the plants and animals you imagine.

____

____

____

Check Your Own Work

Choose a piece of writing from your writing portfolio, a work in progress, an assignment from another class, or a letter. Revise it, using the skills you have reviewed. This checklist will help you.

- ✔ Have you correctly used an adjective that tells exactly how many or about how many?
- ✔ Did you use the correct form of the adjective when you were comparing two or more things?
- ✔ Did you use the correct demonstrative adjective to show whether nouns are near or far?

Name .... Date ....

78 Adverbs

An **adverb** tells more about a verb. Some adverbs tell when, where, or how something happens. Many adverbs end in *ly*.

WHEN	**I flew my kite today.**
WHERE	**The kite flew high in the air.**
HOW	**I ran quickly across the field.**

A **Look at each verb in italics. Underline the adverb that tells more about that verb.**

1. Many choices you *make* today help you and others enjoy good health.
2. Germs from a sneeze *spread* easily to your hands, but you can sneeze into the crook of your arm.
3. Owen *brushes* his teeth thoroughly.
4. Rosario *washes* her hands often.
5. Good feelings are important for health, so friends who *listen* carefully help us have good health.
6. Promise that we *will exercise* together.
7. When my brothers disagree, they *act* peacefully to solve a problem.
8. When I *speak* kindly to you, we both feel good.
9. The foods we *eat* daily should be fresh and nutritious.
10. Visit a beautiful place and *breathe* deeply.

B **Complete each sentence with an adverb from the list. Use each adverb once.**

always **downstairs** **fast** **patiently** **there**

1. A tornado travels very ________________ .
2. You should ________________ listen for tornado sirens.
3. If you hear one, go ________________ to the basement.
4. Take your pets ________________ with you.
5. Wait ________________ until you hear the "all clear" signal.

Name .... Date ....

79 Adverbs That Tell When or How Often

Adverbs tell more about verbs. Some adverbs tell when or how often an action happens.

Nicholas *read* yesterday.

Underline the adverbs that tell when. The verbs are in italics.

1. Thomas Gallaudet *was born* late in the year 1787.
2. He eventually *wanted* to teach deaf people.
3. He soon *went* to France to visit schools for deaf people.
4. When he finally *came* home, he knew how to use sign language.
5. He *traveled* frequently in the United States to raise money for a school.
6. Gallaudet then *founded* the American Asylum for Deaf-Mutes.
7. He *worked* daily to make the school a success.
8. There *had been* no free public school for deaf people before.
9. Because of Gallaudet's efforts, deaf people in the United States now *can receive* an education.
10. Deaf people often *communicate* by using sign language.

Thomas Gallaudet's efforts improved the lives of deaf people in America. Write three sentences describing something you could do to help someone with a disability. Underline all the adverbs.

Name .... Date ....

80 Adverbs That Tell Where

Some adverbs tell where an action takes place.

***Search* <u>everywhere</u> on the Internet.**

A **Underline the adverbs that tell where. The verbs are in italics.**

1. Do not *stand* up at the computer.
2. *Type* in a keyword or topic.
3. *Press* down on the enter key to begin a search.
4. *Discover* useful links below the search box.
5. *Scroll* down for more links.
6. *Scroll* up for the most relevant links.
7. *Look* away from the screen to rest your eyes.
8. *Print* out related information.
9. *Skim* and *scan* everywhere to gather information.
10. *Save* your notes here.

B **Complete each sentence with an adverb listed below. Use each adverb once.**

close inside on out here

1. Beekeepers build hives ____________ in our town.
2. Beekeeping is seldom done ____________ to a house.
3. When beekeepers check the hives, they rarely look ____________ .
4. A beekeeper lifts a frame ____________ of the hive to collect the honey.
5. A bee makes only one teaspoon of honey during its whole life, no matter how many flowers it lands ____________ .

Name .... Date ....

81 Adverbs That Tell How

Some adverbs tell how an action takes place.

Scientists *gather* information carefully.

A **Underline the adverbs that tell how. The verbs are in italics.**

1. A zoologist in the National Zoo *observes* pandas quietly.
2. The information *is charted* expertly.
3. Zoologists *learn* about pandas quickly.
4. They help pandas *live* contentedly.
5. Feeding *is* precisely *monitored*.
6. The scientists expertly *plan* the feeding schedules.
7. For an unhappy panda, a zoologist slowly *changes* the environment.
8. Zoologists carefully *improve* the situation.
9. The zoo team thoroughly *evaluates* each change.
10. Pandas *munch* happily on bamboo.

B **Circle the verb. Write the adverb that tells how.**

_______________ 1. Jack carefully emptied his fish tank.

_______________ 2. Nervously, the fish swam in a bowl.

_______________ 3. Slowly, Jack scrubbed the tank clean.

_______________ 4. He refilled the tank neatly.

_______________ 5. Jack gently placed the fish in its tank.

Adverbs & Conjunctions

Name .... Date ....

82 More Adverbs

An **adverb** tells more about a verb. Adverbs can tell when, where, or how something happens.

WHEN	**I went bird watching yesterday.**
WHERE	**There is a bird sanctuary nearby.**
HOW	**Most birds fly quickly.**

A **Underline the adverb in each sentence. Does it tell when, where, or how? Write *when, where,* or *how* on the line.**

_______________ 1. People everywhere like to watch birds.

_______________ 2. Bird watchers get up early.

_______________ 3. They go outside and visit a field or forest.

_______________ 4 They walk quietly.

_______________ 5. They listen carefully for any sounds.

_______________ 6. They look around, checking for any movement.

_______________ 7. They wait patiently to see different birds.

_______________ 8. They try never to frighten the birds.

_______________ 9. Bird watchers often keep lists of the birds they see.

_______________ 10. Sometimes they take pictures of the birds.

B **Complete each sentence to make it true about you. Use an adverb that tells when, where, or how. Choose adverbs from the list or use your own ideas.**

always fast never often slowly untidily
carefully inside noisily outdoors sometimes upstairs

when 1. I _______________ do my homework on time.

how 2. I eat _______________.

where 3. I like to play games _______________.

how 4. I do my math problems _______________.

when 5. In the evening I _______________ play video games.

Name .... Date ....

83 Negatives

A negative idea is formed in several ways. You can add *not* to the verb. You can add *not* as part of a contraction: *didn't, wasn't, can't*. You can add *never* before the verb. Because *not* and *never* tell about verbs, they are adverbs.

Casey is not careless.

She doesn't ride her bike without a helmet.

She never leaves her bike in the driveway.

Be careful to use only one negative word in a sentence.

INCORRECT	**She doesn't never forget to signal.**
CORRECT	**She doesn't forget to signal.**
CORRECT	**She never forgets to signal.**

A Underline the negative word in each sentence.

1. The experiment wasn't easy to do.
2. We had never tried to make paper before.
3. We did not know how to begin.
4. The instructions weren't clear.
5. We didn't know it would make such a mess.

B Find the sentences that are incorrect. Write them correctly. Some of the sentences are correct.

1. My cousin won't play outside when it's cold.

____

2. He doesn't never ice skate.

____

3. He can't ski.

____

4. He does not never make snowmen.

____

5. He isn't never happy in the winter.

____

Name .... Date ....

84 *Good* and *Well*

Good is an **adjective** that describes a noun.

A good symbol is easy to recognize.

Well is an **adverb** that tells about verbs.

Numbers are symbols that serve us well.

Circle the correct word in parentheses.

1. (Good Well) signs tell people when to use caution.
2. Roads near schools should be marked (good well).
3. Stop signs are (good well) for safety.
4. It is (good well) to know that blue road signs offer information.
5. A picture with a red slash through it is a (good well) way to show that something is not allowed.
6. The poison symbol is a (good well) reminder to keep something out of the reach of children.
7. The color red works (good well) to warn us of danger.
8. People who do not speak the same language can communicate (good well) by using symbols.
9. The eagle is a (good well) symbol for our country.
10. Chris is (good well) at looking for a recycling symbol on cans.
11. Sign language works (good well) for many deaf people.
12. Musical notes are (good well) symbols for recording music.
13. Morse code was once (good well) for communicating a message.
14. (Good Well) secret codes can be hard to decode.
15. A handshake is a (good well) sign of hello or good-bye.

eat S w coat i r larg eye t

Adverbs & Conjunctions

Name .... Date ....

85 *To, Too,* and *Two*

To tells where, or it means "until."

Mrs. Lauer's class took a trip to the forest preserve.

Too means "also" or "more than enough."

Many parents went on the trip too.

Two means "the number 2."

The class was at the forest preserve for two hours.

A Circle *to, too,* or *two* to correctly complete each sentence.

1. One group went (to too two) the playground and collected trash.
2. A different group started working at 10 minutes (to too two) nine.
3. The parents helped with the cleanup (to too two).
4. Each group collected (to too two) bags of trash.
5. One bag of trash was (to too two) heavy.
6. Everyone went (to too two) the picnic area for lunch.
7. Parents brought (to too two) sandwiches for each child.
8. The class went (to too two) the riverbank after lunch.
9. While at the preserve, Rosi saw (to too two) cardinals.
10. Let's clean up the school playground (to too two)!

B Complete each sentence with the word *to, too,* or *two.*

1. Air and water are ________ natural resources.
2. Soil is a natural resource ________ .
3. Trash that is not recycled is taken________ a landfill.
4. Recycling and reusing are ________ ways that natural resources can be protected.
5. Leaves and grass clippings can be taken ________ a compost center.

Adverbs & Conjunctions

Name .... Date ....

86 *Their* and *There*

Their tells who owns something. *Their* is an adjective.

César Chávez and his family picked fruit to earn their money.

There usually means "in that place." *There* is an adverb.

They lived there.

Complete each sentence with *there* or *their.*

1. Business people who own large farms need people to work __________ .
2. César Chávez saw a need for better conditions for the migrant workers who worked __________.
3. Traveling workers pick fruit and vegetables for __________ wages.
4. Chávez worked to improve __________ working conditions.
5. __________ pay was too low for the hours they worked.
6. He protested the use of pesticides that poisoned the workers and __________ children.
7. In California and Arizona, he went without eating food for days to call attention to __________ cause.
8. Many groups __________ and in other states supported his work.
9. He spent his money to organize workers __________ on the farms.
10. Chávez created the United Farm Workers to work toward improving __________ wages and other benefits.

César Chávez continued his efforts to make sure migrant workers were given their rights. Give an example of how you kept working to complete a difficult task.

Name .... Date ....

87 Coordinating Conjunctions

A **coordinating conjunction** joins two words or groups of words. The words *and, but,* and *or* are coordinating conjunctions.

AND **Cows *and* chickens are farm animals.**

BUT **Cows are large *but* gentle.**

OR **Chickens are raised for eggs *or* for meat.**

A Circle the coordinating conjunction in each sentence. Underline the words or groups of words the coordinating conjunction joins.

1. Fruits and vegetables are grown on farms.
2. Some farmers grow wheat or soybeans.
3. Most farmers don't work with horses or with oxen.
4. Now they have tractors and harvesters.
5. Their equipment is expensive but necessary.

B Write the coordinating conjunction that makes sense in each sentence.

and but or

1. Animals are kept in barns __________ in pens.
2. Farmers feed __________ water their animals.
3. Farmers milk cows with machines __________ by hand.
4. Cheese __________ ice cream are made from milk.
5. A farmer's job is difficult __________ rewarding.

Name .... Date ....

88 Reviewing Adverbs

A **Circle the adverbs. The verbs are in italics.**

1. The people from New York *waved* wildly at the passing parade.
2. Marching bands from Iowa *played* well.
3. The florist *displayed* the colorful flowers beautifully.
4. Huge balloons *soared* grandly on long strings.
5. Expert riders *groomed* the parade horses neatly.

B **Circle the correct adverb in parentheses.**

6. (Tomorrow Yesterday) I met an author at the mall.
7. The author Christine McDonnell has (early often) visited bookstores.
8. I have (already ever) read several of her books.
9. Our teacher (sometimes early) shares her stories with us.
10. Mrs. Hughes read *Toad Food and Measle Soup* (today tomorrow).

C **Circle the adverbs. The verbs are in italics.**

11. Please *carry* the groceries inside.
12. The bags *tumbled* down from the table.
13. *Take* the shampoo upstairs.
14. The phone bill *is* near.
15. We *looked* everywhere for the lost car keys.

D **Circle each adverb. On the line write if it tells *when, where,* or *how.***

__________ 16. Local produce is packaged loosely.

__________ 17. Fresh tomatoes are here.

__________ 18. Farmers depend on selling crops locally.

__________ 19. People buy fresh vegetables carefully.

__________ 20. Stores prefer to stock fresh fruit daily.

Continued →

Name .... Date ....

E **Complete each sentence with *good* or *well*.**

21. Consumers must make __________ choices.
22. __________ shoppers consider the quality and the cost of an item.
23. Products from other countries often sell __________ if similar products are not made locally.
24. __________ products made locally can be sold overseas.
25. A product that is made __________ can be the best deal.

F **Circle the coordinating conjunction in each sentence. Underline the words or groups of words the coordinating conjunction joins.**

26. Turtles live in water that is salty or fresh.
27. They use flippers or feet to swim.
28. Not every turtle can pull in its head and legs.
29. Turtles eat plants and insects.
30. Turtles have skin that is tough-looking but sensitive.

Try It Yourself

Describe how to make a sandwich in three or more steps. Use adverbs to explain when, where, and how you do each step.

____

____

____

____

Check Your Own Work

Choose a piece of writing from your writing portfolio, a work in progress, an assignment from another class, or a letter. Revise it, using the skills you have reviewed. This checklist will help you.

✔ Have you used adverbs that tell when, where, or how?

✔ Have you used *good* as an adjective and *well* as an adverb?

Name .... Date ....

89 End Punctuation

End punctuation makes your sentences clear and signals the kind of sentence you are writing. A sentence that tells something ends with a **period.**

The sun is a star.

A sentence that asks a question ends with a **question mark.**

How hot is the sun?

A sentence that expresses strong or sudden feeling ends with an **exclamation point.**

Wow, that's hot!

Place the correct mark of punctuation at the end of each sentence. On the line write *S* if the sentence is a statement, *Q* if it is a question, or *E* if it is an exclamation.

_____ 1. Plants use energy from the sun

_____ 2. Sunspots are dark patches on the sun

_____ 3. How do animals use the sun

_____ 4. Wow, the eclipse was incredible

_____ 5. Stars are hot balls of gas

_____ 6. Planets are not as hot as the sun

_____ 7. Why do planets orbit the sun

_____ 8. Asteroids also orbit the sun

_____ 9. Telescopes help us see objects in space

_____ 10. What makes up the tail of a comet

_____ 11. Astronomers are scientists who study planets

_____ 12. Did you know they also study asteroids and meteors

_____ 13. There is much to discover about our solar system

_____ 14. Astronomers are amazing

_____ 15. I want to become one

Name .... Date ....

90 Capitalization—Part I

The first word of a sentence always begins with a capital letter.

A first-aid kit is important to have when camping.

Names of people and pets begin with a capital letter.

Catherine **Barney** **Fido**

Names of streets, cities, states, and countries begin with capital letters.

First Avenue **Boston** **Texas** **Mexico**

The proofreading mark (≡) is used under a letter to show that it should be capitalized.

portland, oregon, gets about 40 inches of rain each year.
≡ ≡

A **Use the proofreading symbol (≡) to show which letters should be capitalized.**

1. mexico has many earthquakes.
2. raquel's pet, blanco, was frightened in the last quake.
3. the buildings on first street were damaged.
4. people in california prepare for earthquakes.
5. india has also seen natural disasters.
6. rosina once survived a great storm in bombay, india.
7. many people in china have lived through floods.
8. ching lee saw floods in nanjing, china.
9. he now lives on university drive in fargo.
10. there he must deal with north dakota's blizzards.

B **Use the proofreading symbol (≡) to show which letters should be capitalized.**

El Niño is a warm current of water in the pacific ocean. it affects the weather from the united states to south africa. El Niño might cause indira thali's family in madras, india, to live through drought and juan ruiz's home in lima, peru, to flood.

Name .... Date ....

91 Capitalization—Part II

Days of the week and months of the year begin with capital letters.

Tuesday **August**

Holidays begin with capital letters.

Kwanzaa **St. Patrick's Day**

A Use the proofreading symbol (≡) to show which letters should be capitalized.

1. independence day is celebrated on july 4.
2. The parade is scheduled for saturday.
3. Is your vacation in july or august?
4. Does every state celebrate presidents' day?
5. Do we celebrate new year's day on january 1?
6. I have a dentist appointment thursday afternoon.
7. memorial day is celebrated in may.
8. My brother washes the dishes every monday and wednesday.
9. martin luther king jr. day is a january holiday.
10. Costumes for halloween are in the stores in october.

B Complete each sentence with a holiday, day of the week, or month of the year.

day 1. ________________ comes right after Wednesday.

month 2. Labor Day is in ________________.

holiday 3. In November we get two days off from school for ________________.

month 4. Valentine's Day is celebrated in ________________.

day 5. ________________ is the last school day of the week.

Name .... Date ....

92 Capitalization—Part III

Names of buildings and bridges begin with capital letters.

Empire State Building **Golden Gate Bridge**

The personal pronoun *I* is a capital letter.

My neighbor and I will visit Texas.

A **Use the proofreading symbol (≡) to show which letters should be capitalized.**

1. You will find the library of congress in Washington, D.C.
2. The royal gorge bridge in colorado is the world's highest bridge.
3. The eiffel tower is located in Paris, France.
4. The london tower bridge spans the Thames River in England.
5. Seth and i walked across the golden gate bridge.
6. the visitors enjoyed the art institute of Chicago.
7. my dad works at the willis tower.
8. George Washington did not live in the white house because it was being built when he was president.
9. The betsy ross bridge crosses the Delaware River.
10. This summer i will visit epcot center.

B **Use the proofreading symbol (≡) to show which letters should be capitalized.**

bob and i went sightseeing in boston. we saw the famous faneuil hall. later bob and i walked across the longfellow bridge, which crosses the charles river. we then visited the john f. kennedy library. boston is certainly an exciting city in massachusetts.

Name .... Date ....

93 Abbreviations

An **abbreviation** is a short form of a word. Abbreviations for addresses begin with capital letters and usually end with periods.

Street	**St.**	**Place**	**Pl.**

Abbreviations for units of measure do not begin with capital letters.

foot	**ft.**	**inch**	**in.**

Oak Rd.
Pine St.
Elm Ave.

A Write the abbreviation for each underlined word. Use the list below.

Blvd.	**Rd.**	**Dr.**	**Ave.**	**Apt.**
Ln.	**N.**	**St.**	**W.**	**Pkwy.**

1. Seventh Avenue ____________
2. Lincoln Parkway ____________
3. North Elm Street ____________
4. Addison Boulevard ____________
5. Lakeview Drive ____________
6. Miller Road ____________
7. Montgomery Lane ____________
8. Apartment 3B ____________
9. Orange Street ____________
10. West Ott Road ____________

B Write the unit of measure for each abbreviation. Use the list below.

quart	**pound**	**inch**	**pint**	**second**
mile	**yard**	**gallon**	**minute**	**ounce**

1. oz. ________________________
2. sec. ________________________
3. in. ________________________
4. qt. ________________________
5. gal. ________________________
6. min. ________________________
7. pt. ________________________
8. mi. ________________________
9. lb. ________________________
10. yd. ________________________

Name .... Date ....

Punctuation, Capitalization & Abbreviations

94 More Abbreviations

Days of the week and some months of the year can be abbreviated.

MONTHS Do not abbreviate *May, June,* and *July*.

Abbreviate *September* using the first four letters of the word.

Abbreviate the rest of the months using the first three letters of each word.

DAYS Abbreviate *Tuesday* using the first four letters of the word.

Abbreviate *Thursday* using the first five letters of the word.

Abbreviate the rest of the days using the first three letters of each word.

A **Write the abbreviation for each month that has an abbreviation.**

1. April ____________
2. February ____________
3. November ____________
4. January ____________
5. June ____________
6. March ____________
7. July ____________
8. September ____________
9. October ____________
10. December ____________

B **Write the correct day of the week on the line. In parentheses write the abbreviation.**

1. The day that comes in the middle of the school week is ______________ (__________).
2. The day before that is ______________ (__________).
3. The last day of the school week is ______________ (__________).
4. The day after that is ______________ (__________).
5. The first day of the school week is ______________ (__________).

Name .... Date ....

95 Personal Titles and Initials

Titles and names can also be abbreviated. *Mr.* is an abbreviated title for a man. *Ms.* and *Mrs.* are abbreviated titles for a woman. Each abbreviation begins with a capital letter and ends with a period.

Doctor Roger John Kugel **Dr. R. J. Kugel**

A **Match the words in Column A with the abbreviations in Column B. Some letters will be used twice.**

	COLUMN A	COLUMN B
______	1. a leader of a state	a. Mr.
______	2. a married man	b. Dr.
______	3. a doctor	c. Capt.
______	4. a head of a school	d. Gov.
______	5. a person in charge of a ship	e. Prin.
______	6. a single man	f. Rev.
______	7. a single or married woman	g. Mrs.
______	8. a married woman	h. Ms.
______	9. reverend (a religious leader)	
______	10. a dentist	

B **Rewrite each name with the correct title before it. Use capital letters and periods correctly.**

1. susanna b barnes (married woman) ______________________________
2. irene j cordova (single woman) ______________________________
3. john r lee (governor) ______________________________
4. h r brown (doctor) ______________________________
5. caryn j roberts (boat captain) ______________________________

Punctuation, Capitalization & Abbreviations

Name .... Date ....

96 Titles of Books and Poems

There are special rules when writing the titles of books and poems. Titles of books are underlined when handwritten.

A River Ran Wild by Lynne Cherry

Titles of poems have quotation marks around them.

"An Elephant Is Hard to Hide" by Jack Prelutsky

A Write on the line whether each title is for a book or a poem.

_____________ 1. Charlie and the Chocolate Factory

_____________ 2. "Getting Dressed for School"

_____________ 3. "A Bug Sat on a Silver Flower"

_____________ 4. The Boxcar Children

_____________ 5. Ramona Quimby, Age 8

_____________ 6. "The Early Bird"

_____________ 7. Charlotte's Web

_____________ 8. Through Grandpa's Eyes

_____________ 9. The Greedy Triangle

_____________ 10. "If I Were Ruler of the World"

B Underline or place quotation marks where necessary.

1. The Best Christmas Pageant Ever (a book by Barbara Robinson)
2. An Early Worm Got Out of Bed (a poem by Jack Prelutsky)
3. The Last Dragon (a book by Susan Miho Nunes)
4. Bridge to Terabithia (a book by Katherine Paterson)
5. Tree House (a poem by Shel Silverstein)

Name .... Date ....

97 More Titles of Books and Poems

Each important word in a title begins with a capital letter. The first word and the last word of a title always begin with a capital letter. A short word such as *of, to, for, a, an,* or *the* is not capitalized unless it is the first or last word in the title.

The Spy on Third (book)

"And the Green Grass Grew All Around" (poem)

A **Rewrite the titles, using capital letters where needed. Write whether each is a book or a poem.**

__________ 1. chang and the bamboo flute by Elizabeth Starr Hill

____

__________ 2. ben and me by Robert Lawson

____

__________ 3. "if once you have slept on an island" by Rachel Field

____

__________ 4. "every time i climb a tree" by David McCord

____

__________ 5. elisa in the middle by Johanna Hurwitz

____

B **Write each title correctly.**

1. the owl and the pussycat (poem)

____

2. beans on the roof (book)

____

3. clever polly and the stupid wolf (book)

____

4. the midnight ride of paul revere (poem)

____

5. when i was young in the mountains (book)

____

Name .... Date ....

98 Commas in a Series

Three or more words or groups of words of the same kind written one after another are called a **series.** Often parts of the series are connected by the coordinating conjunction *and* or *or.* Commas are used to separate words in a series.

Light, heat, and sound are forms of energy.

Did a person, an animal, or a thing make that sound?

Rewrite each sentence. Add commas to separate the items in series.

1. Trucks planes and motorcycles make loud sounds.

____

2. Dripping rain purring cats and blowing leaves make soft sounds.

____

3. A bird a kitten or a small bell make a high sound.

____

4. Lions cows and bears make low sounds.

____

5. People can make sounds by shaking hitting or blowing into musical instruments.

____

6. We shake maracas rattles and tambourines to make sounds.

____

7. You can make sounds by hitting a drum a triangle or a gong.

____

8. They blow into harmonicas recorders and horns to make sounds.

____

9. People also use their lips teeth and tongues to make sounds.

____

10. The outer ear the eardrum and the inner ear help us hear sounds.

____

Name .... Date ....

99 Commas in Direct Address

Speaking directly to a person and using that person's name is called **direct address.** Commas are used to separate the name of the person spoken to from the rest of the sentence.

Turn on the light, Thomas Edison.

Please, Louis Braille, read these dots.

Insert one or more commas to separate the name of the person spoken to from the rest of the sentence.

1. Take a picture George Eastman.
2. Thanks for the stuffed toy Ms. Steiff.
3. Launch the rocket Robert Goddard.
4. Mary Anderson wipe the windshield.
5. Play ball Alexander Cartwright!
6. Benjamin Banneker water the crops.
7. Find the computer bug Grace Hopper.
8. Check out a library book Melvil Dewey.
9. Laszlo Biro please hand me that ballpoint pen.
10. These books Mr. Gutenberg are printed beautifully.
11. Please answer the phone Alexander Graham Bell.
12. Helicopters Igor Sikorsky are amazing flying machines.
13. Benjamin Franklin let's go to the public library.
14. The light bulb Joseph Swan is a remarkable invention.
15. Let's make more of everything Mr. Ford.
16. Find hundreds of uses for peanuts George Washington Carver.
17. Inventors Jean are important to all of us.
18. Do you realize Andy what Eli Whitney accomplished?
19. Kathleen what is your favorite invention?
20. Name something Mr. Hartfield that you could not do if there were no inventors.

Name .... Date ....

100 Commas in Compound Sentences

A comma is used when two short sentences are combined into one longer sentence. This longer sentence is called a **compound sentence.** To make a compound sentence, use a comma followed by *and, but,* or *or.*

We get together for Thanksgiving, and we cook a big meal.
I like other holidays, but Thanksgiving is my favorite.
We will watch a football game, or we will go for a walk.

Combine each pair of sentences into a compound sentence. Use a comma and *and, but,* or *or.*

1. Matt made the stuffing. Allison put it into the turkey.

 ____

2. Chris whipped the potatoes. They were still lumpy.

 ____

3. Elizabeth set the table. Jason arranged the flowers.

 ____

4. Sylvia peeled the onions. She cooked them in cream.

 ____

5. Before dinner we might watch a video. We might play outdoors.

 ____

6. Katie wanted to slice the carrots. She couldn't find a knife.

 ____

7. Aaron made the salad. Ann made the salad dressing.

 ____

8. Nicky called us to dinner. I didn't hear her at first.

 ____

9. The dinner was delicious. Everyone ate a lot.

 ____

10. We'll eat the leftovers later. We'll save them for tomorrow.

 ____

Name .... Date ....

101 Apostrophes

An **apostrophe** is a punctuation mark used in several different ways. An apostrophe is used to form the possessive of a noun.

The boy has a hat. The boy's hat is blue.
The girls have hats. The girls' hats are red.
The women have hats. The women's hats are yellow.

An apostrophe is also used to replace the letters left out in a contraction.

He is not coming because he cannot find his hat.
He isn't coming because he can't find his hat.

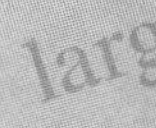

Rewrite each sentence. Add apostrophes where necessary.

1. Carlas homework isnt done.

   ____

2. The childrens lunches arent ready.

   ____

3. The two dogs werent fed.

   ____

4. Both dogs collars were missing.

   ____

5. Dads toast wasnt hot.

   ____

6. Mom couldnt unzip the babies diaper bags.

   ____

7. My three brothers shoes shouldnt be on the stairs.

   ____

8. Henry cant find Miltons jacket.

   ____

9. My familys day didnt start out well.

   ____

10. I hope tomorrow wont be like today.

   ____

Name .... Date ....

102 Addresses

In an address capitalize the first letter of every word and abbreviation. Capitalize both letters of a state abbreviation. A comma always separates the city and the state, but there is no comma between the state abbreviation and the ZIP code. If there is an apartment, suite, or floor number, it is separated from the rest of the address by a comma.

Ms. Karen Briggs
231 S. Banks St., Apt. 14
Columbus, OH 43203

Dr. Charles Drew
62 Hampton Rd., Suite 6A
Alexandria, VA 39532

Rewrite each address, using capital letters and commas where needed.

1. mr. oscar perez ____________________
   2641 tijeras st. ____________________
   beaumont tx 77707 ____________________
2. mrs. clair pinkney ____________________
   328 w. broad st. apt. 6C ____________________
   spokane wa 99205 ____________________
3. dr. laura lin ____________________
   33 oakley rd. suite 12 ____________________
   bangor me 04401 ____________________
4. gov. hector ryan ____________________
   632 peach st. ____________________
   atlanta ga 30303 ____________________
5. capt. ann rosen ____________________
   4656 crescent court ____________________
   reno nv 89506 ____________________

Name .... Date ....

103 Direct Quotations

A **direct quotation** contains the exact words a person says. Use a comma to separate what is said from the rest of the sentence. Place quotation marks before and after the words of a speaker.

Pam said, "There were 13 original colonies."

"You are correct," stated the quizmaster.

A **Put commas and quotation marks in the correct places.**

1. Connecticut was one of the 13 colonies announced the tour guide.
2. The Gullah people are important to American history explained Mr. Jolie.
3. Ms. Garcia said John Jay worked with George Washington.
4. That is the Liberty Bell whispered a tourist.
5. The colonists opposed the king she said.

B **Rewrite each sentence, using quotation marks, commas, and capital letters.**

1. Let's visit Colonial Williamsburg begged the class.

   ____

2. Ms. scadron said we can see how people once lived in virginia.

   ____

3. joseph continued they have a fife-and-drum parade.

   ____

4. We can eat colonial food replied arthur.

   ____

5. Then let's go to Yorktown suggested michelle.

   ____

Name .... Date ....

104 More Direct Quotations

Sometimes the exact words of a speaker ask a question or express strong feeling. Use a question mark when the exact words are a question. Use an exclamation point when the exact words are an exclamation. The question mark and the exclamation point come before the end quotation marks in direct quotations.

"What's the state bird of Illinois?" asked Sandy.

"It's a cardinal!" exclaimed her cousin.

Put question marks and exclamation points in the correct places. Then add quotation marks to complete the sentences.

1. Did you know that California has a state animal asked Lily.
2. It's the California grizzly bear yelled Eliza.
3. Look at all the bluebonnets exclaimed Mark.
4. Why are there so many bluebonnets in Texas asked Shoshanna.
5. Evan asked Is the dogwood of Virginia a flower or a tree
6. It's both shouted Pia.
7. What do you think the state beverage is in Florida asked Maria.
8. Ned shouted Orange juice, of course
9. Alaska has fine salmon cried the warden.
10. Is it the state fish asked the tourist.
11. Would you like to visit the Empire State Building asked the guide.
12. You are lucky to live near Mount Rushmore yelled Marlene.
13. Let's swim in the Great Salt Lake shouted Natalia.
14. The wind is howling across the plains shrieked Linda.
15. Kenisha asked Have you been to Niagara Falls

Name .... Date ....

105 Reviewing Punctuation, Capitalization & Abbreviations

A **Write the abbreviation for each word.**

1. Sunday ____________
2. Friday ____________
3. Saturday ____________
4. Wednesday ____________
5. Monday ____________
6. April ____________
7. August ____________
8. September ____________
9. October ____________
10. November ____________
11. Thursday ____________
12. Tuesday ____________
13. yard ____________
14. gallon ____________
15. Boulevard ____________
16. December ____________
17. doctor ____________
18. married woman ____________
19. single or married woman ____________
20. single or married man ____________

B **Write the proofreading symbol (≡) under the letters that should be capitalized.**

21. mary lives at 3040 wellington street.
22. Our family has a picnic on memorial day.
23. we saw the oakland bay bridge in the distance.
24. The empire state building is in new york city.
25. ann moved to chicago, illinois.

C **Put commas in the correct places and put the correct mark of punctuation at the end of each sentence.**

26. Is this your music Ludwig von Beethoven
27. Georgia O'Keeffe what gorgeous flowers you paint
28. Will you blow the trumpet Louis Armstrong
29. Balance your mobile Alexander Calder
30. Wolfgang Amadeus Mozart your music is magnificent

Continued →

D **Put commas, quotation marks, question marks, and exclamation points in the correct places.**

31. Mrs. Carr asked Do you like popcorn
32. Dennis exclaimed It's my favorite snack
33. Did you know that most popcorn is grown in the Midwest asked Mrs. Carr.
34. Ohio Iowa Illinois and Indiana are all popcorn producers added Jeff.
35. Jeanne shouted Popcorn is ready

Try It Yourself

What famous person in history do you wish you could talk to on the telephone? Write a question you would ask and how the person might reply. Use quotation marks, commas, question marks, and exclamation points correctly.

____

____

____

____

____

Check Your Own Work

Choose a piece of writing from your writing portfolio, a work in progress, an assignment from another class, or a letter. Revise it, using the skills you have reviewed. This checklist will help you.

- ✔ Did you end each sentence with the correct punctuation mark?
- ✔ Have you followed the rules for commas?
- ✔ Did you use quotation marks before and after speakers' words?
- ✔ Have you capitalized all proper nouns?
- ✔ Have you spelled abbreviations correctly?

Name .... Date ....

106 Subjects and Predicates

A **diagram** is a drawing that shows how the parts of a sentence go together. The most important parts of a sentence are the subject and the predicate. The simple subject of a sentence is usually a noun or a subject pronoun. The simple predicate of a sentence is the verb.

In a sentence diagram, the simple subject and the simple predicate go on a horizontal line (a line that goes across). The subject is at the left, and the predicate is at the right. A vertical line (a line that goes up and down) separates them.

SENTENCE: **Fish swim.**

Fish	**swim**

Diagramming

Diagram each of these sentences.

1. Babies cry.

2. Linda shouted.

3. We won.

4. Bees buzz.

Continued →

Name .... Date ....

5. Jake ran.

6. She cooks.

7. Eagles fly.

8. Dad sang.

9. Kittens purr.

10. I skated.

Name .... Date ....

107 Possessives

In a diagram, a possessive noun is written on a slanted line under the noun it goes with. The possessive adjectives *my, your, his, her, its, our,* and *their* are diagrammed the same way.

SENTENCE: Karen's puppy wiggled.

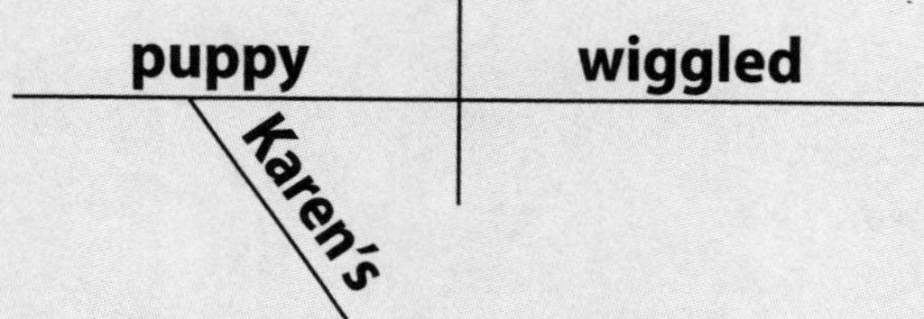

Diagram each of these sentences.

1. My balloon burst.

2. Jack's roses bloomed.

3. Our roof leaks.

Continued →

Name .... Date ....

4. Mom's canary sings.

5. Their team lost.

6. Maya's phone rang.

7. His kite flew.

8. Rabbits' ears twitch.

Name .... Date ....

108 Adjectives

In a diagram, an adjective is written on a slanted line under the noun it tells about.

SENTENCE: Shiny trumpets blared.

Diagram each of these sentences.

1. Many stars twinkled.

2. Hungry wolves prowl.

3. Funny things happened.

4. The wind blew.

Continued →

Name .... Date ....

5. Big waves crashed.

6. Cool rain fell.

7. Angry bees sting.

8. The children played.

9. Little chicks peeped.

10. Two puppies slept.

Name .... Date ....

109 Adverbs

In a diagram, an adverb is written on a slanted line under the verb it tells more about.

SENTENCE: The crowd cheered loudly.

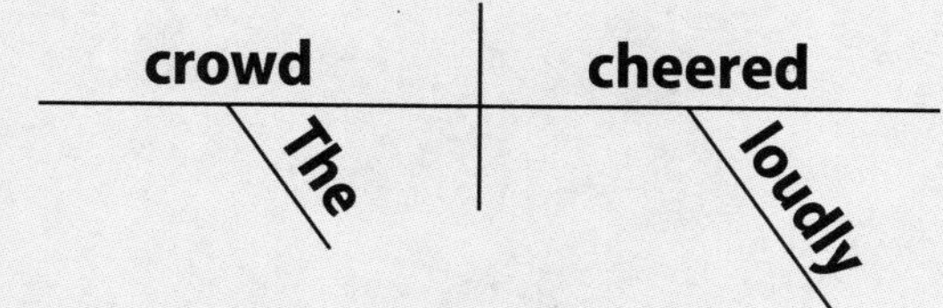

Diagram each of these sentences.

1. Our team played well.

2. The bird chirped sweetly.

3. Good cooks measure carefully.

4. Monkeys chatter noisily.

Diagramming

Continued →

Name .... Date ....

5. Monica's class worked hard.

6. The contest ends tomorrow.

7. The train raced forward.

8. My mother sews beautifully.

9. Bill's horse jumped gracefully.

10. The teakettle whistles loudly.

Name .... Date ....

110 Adjectives as Subject Complements

In a diagram, an adjective used as a subject complement is written on the horizontal line to the right of the being verb. A slanted line that points back at the subject separates the adjective from the being verb.

SENTENCE: My dad is tall.

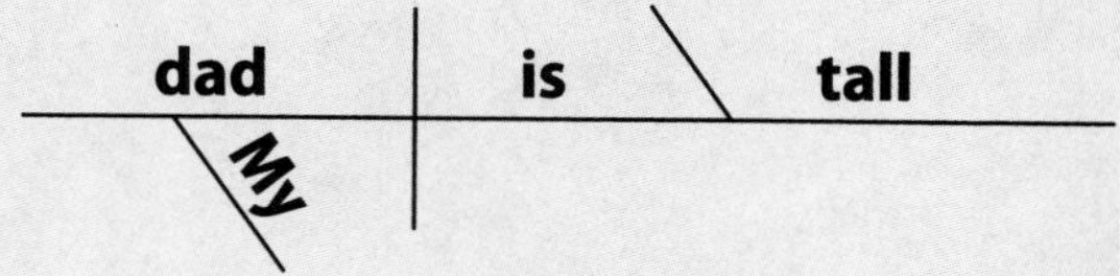

Diagrammming

Diagram each of these sentences.

1. The soup is delicious.

2. That game was easy.

3. Tom's band is terrific.

4. The room was dark.

Continued →

Name .... Date ....

5. Their song was wonderful.

6. The beach was empty.

7. The sand was hot.

8. Jesse's skateboard is new.

9. My cousins are friendly.

10. Some storms are dangerous.

Name .... Date ....

111 Compound Subjects

A compound subject is when a sentence has more than one subject. The subjects are usually joined by the word *and.* In the sentence below, both *kittens* and *puppies* are the subjects.

SENTENCE: Kittens and puppies are cute.

In a diagram, each subject in a compound subject goes on a separate horizontal line. A dashed line for the conjunction connects the subject lines.

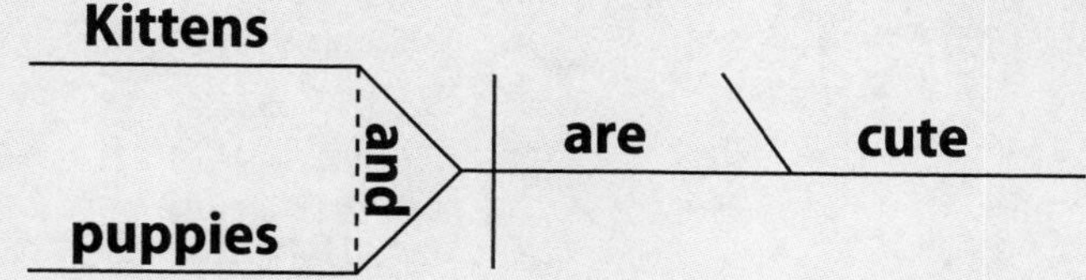

Diagram each of these sentences.

1. Mark and Nina swim well.

2. Barry and I ran fast.

3. Plums and peaches are sweet.

4. Mom and Dad worked hard.

Continued →

Name .... Date ....

5. Ana and Diego are tired.

6. Lions and cheetahs run quickly.

7. She and Toby were happy.

8. Cars and trucks stopped nearby.

9. Carol and Ned sang loudly.

10. Fritz and Sandy were proud.

Diagramming

Name .... Date ....

112 Compound Predicates

In a diagram, each verb in a compound predicate goes on a separate horizontal line. A dashed line for the conjunction connects the simple predicates.

SENTENCE: My brother rides and ropes.

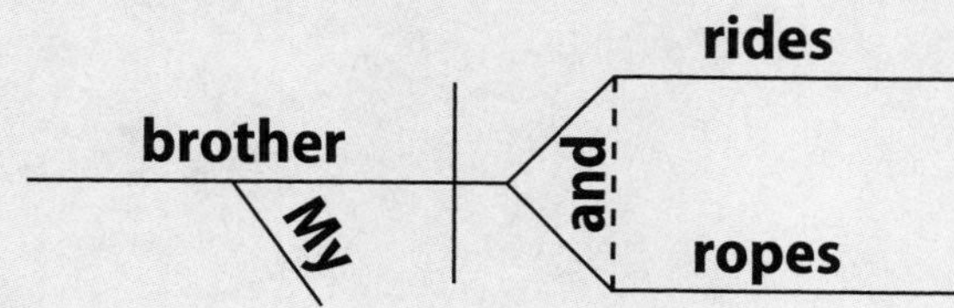

Diagram each of these sentences.

1. Corrine's hamster eats and plays.

2. Careful writers plan and edit.

3. The audience whistled and clapped.

Diagramming

Continued →

Name .... Date ....

4. Loud thunder cracked and boomed.

5. The player shoots and scores.

6. Leland's mother draws and paints.

7. The dancer tripped and fell.

8. Our teacher jokes and laughs.

Name .... Date ....

113 Compound Complements

In a diagram, each adjective in a compound subject complement goes on a separate horizontal line. A dashed line for the conjunction connects the subject complements.

SENTENCE: The children were tired but happy.

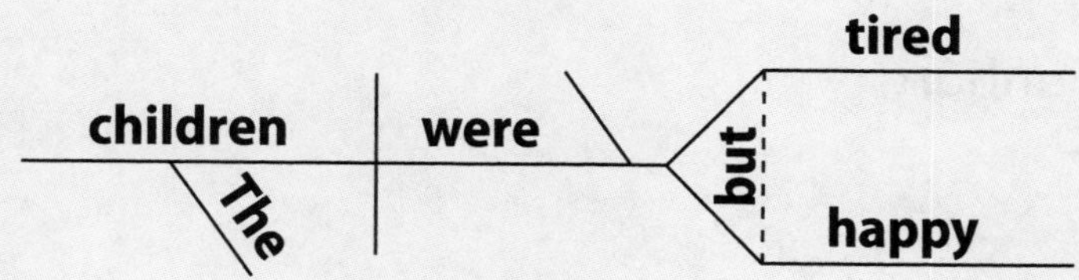

Diagram each of these sentences.

1. This mystery is funny and exciting.

2. Bella's aunt is tall and thin.

3. The parade was long and colorful.

4. His bike is old and rusty.

Continued →

Name .... Date ....

5. The pizza was hot and spicy.

6. Kevin's dog was filthy but unhurt.

7. The game was long and boring.

8. Their boat was green and blue.

9. The salad was tasty and nutritious.

10. My ferret is cute and playful.

Name .... Date ....

114 Compound Sentences

To diagram a compound sentence, diagram each sentence separately, one above the other. Connect the sentences with a dashed vertical line at the left of the sentences. Write the conjunction on the dashed line.

SENTENCE: My brother walked slowly, but I ran.

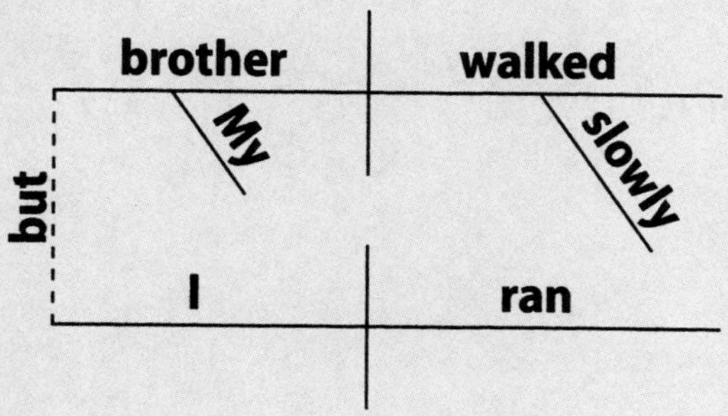

brother | walked
My
slowly
but
I | ran

Diagram each of these sentences.

1. The cake is delicious, but the milk is sour.

2. The game was exciting, and we won easily.

3. The rain stopped, and the children ran outside.

Continued →

Name .... Date ....

4. The woods were quiet, and everyone slept soundly.

5. My brother works hard, but my sister is lazy.

6. The lion roared, and the clown ran away.

7. The movie was scary, and Melanie screamed.

8. The water was warm, and Jacob jumped in.

Name .... Date ....

115 Diagramming Practice

In a diagram, the subject, the verb, and the subject complement go on the horizontal line. Possessives, adjectives, and adverbs go on slanted lines under the words they tell about.

SENTENCE: My uncle was angry yesterday.

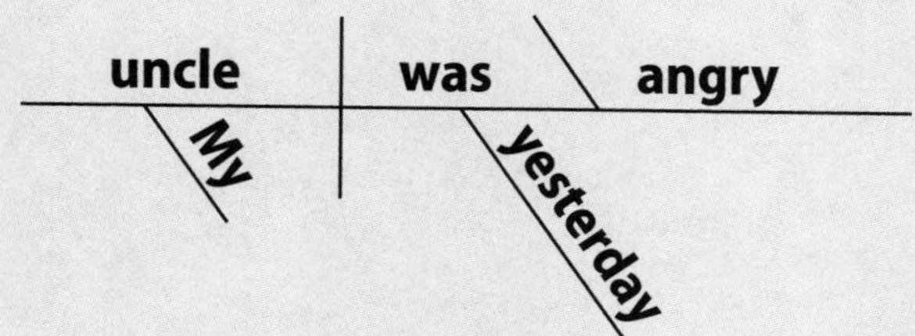

Diagram each of these sentences.

1. Jen's painting is beautiful.

2. The ice melted quickly.

3. Funny clowns walked backward.

4. Her movements were graceful.

Diagramming

Continued →

Name .... Date ....

5. Old cars are sometimes rusty.

6. The crowd cheered happily.

7. Miguel's brother is strong.

8. Wild horses galloped away.

9. The children were excited.

10. Some mountains are steep.

Diagramming

Name .... Date ....

116 More Diagramming Practice

In a diagram, compound sentence parts go on separate horizontal lines. A dashed line for the conjunction connects the compound parts.

SENTENCE: Gloria and Chan sang and danced.

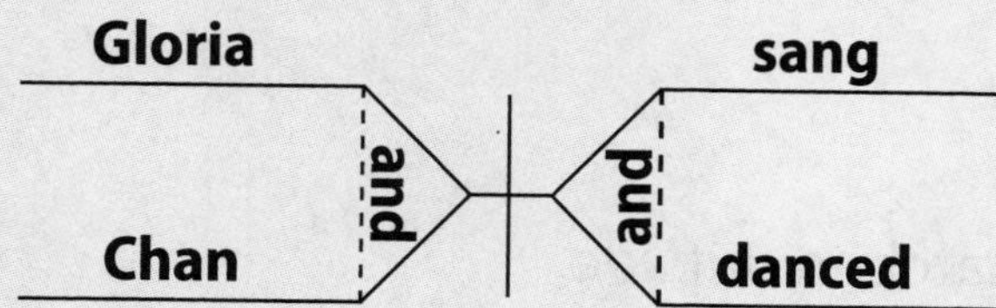

To diagram a compound sentence, diagram each sentence separately, one above the other. Connect the sentences with a dashed line at the left of the sentences. Write the conjunction on the dashed line.

SENTENCE: The sky was gray, and the wind blew hard.

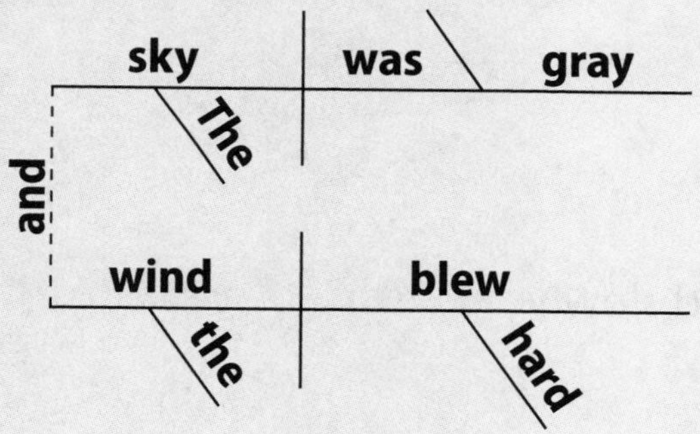

Diagram each of these sentences.

1. The cat and the dog slept peacefully.

2. My sister runs slowly but swims fast.

Continued →

Name .... Date ....

3. That lemonade is cold and delicious.

4. The alarm rang loudly, and we marched outside.

5. The sun was hot, and Marcus walked slowly.

6. Tina waited calmly, but Janet was impatient.

Handbook of Terms

ABBREVIATIONS

An **abbreviation** is a short form of a word. An abbreviation often ends with a period.

- Abbreviations for words in addresses begin with capital letters and end with periods: Ave. = Avenue, Rd. = Road.
- Abbreviations for units of measure do not begin with capital letters: in. = inch, mi. = miles.
- Days of the week and most months of the year can be abbreviated. The abbreviations begin with capital letters and end with periods: Sat. = Saturday, Oct. = October.
- Titles and names can be abbreviated: Dr. M. S. Jones = Doctor Mary Scott Jones.
- State postal abbreviations contain two capital letters and no periods: IL, TX.

ADJECTIVES

An **adjective** is a word that describes or points out a noun.

Articles point out nouns. *A, an,* and *the* are articles: *A* pear and *an* apple are in *the* blue bowl.

Demonstrative adjectives point out specific people, places, or things.

- *This* and *that* point out one person, place, or thing.
- *These* and *those* point out more than one person, place, or thing.
- *This* and *these* point out people, places, or things that are near.
- *That* and *those* point out people, places, or things that are far.

Descriptive adjectives tell about the size, shape, color, weight, age, or other features of nouns.

- A descriptive adjective can come before a noun: *sunny* morning, *hot* day.
- A descriptive adjective that comes after a being verb is a subject complement: The garden was *beautiful.*

- Some adjectives tell how many. They can tell exactly how many *(one, twelve, thirty)* or about how many *(several, few, many, some)*.

Possessive adjectives show possession or ownership. A possessive adjective goes before a noun. The possessive adjectives are *my, your, his, her, its, our,* and *their*: *his* skateboard, *their* bikes.

Proper adjectives are adjectives that come from proper nouns. All other adjectives are called **common adjectives.** A proper adjective begins with a capital letter: *American* history.

See also **Comparisons, Sentences.**

ADVERBS

An **adverb** is a word that tells more about a verb. Many adverbs end in *ly*.

- Some adverbs answer the question *when* or *how often*: It rained *yesterday.* We *usually* eat lunch at noon.
- Some adverbs answer the question *where*: Toshi bent his head *forward.* Sit *here* by the window.
- Some adverbs answer the question *how* or *in what manner*: Jason draws *well.* She dances the waltz *gracefully.*

A negative idea is expressed by using one negative word. This negative word may be *no, not, none, never,* or *nothing*. A sentence should contain only one negative word: I do not have *any* (not *no*) apples.

See also **Comparisons.**

CAPITALIZATION

Many words begin with a capital letter, including the following:

- the first word of a sentence—The bell rang.
- names of people and pets—Did Harry name his owl Hedwig?
- names of streets, cities, states, and countries—Elm Street, Kansas City, Alabama, France
- days of the week and months of the year—Tuesday, June
- holidays—Christmas, Fourth of July

- an abbreviation if the word it stands for begins with a capital letter—Dec. = December, Mon. = Monday
- a title used before a person's name—Mr. Jones, Ms. Marlow
- the first word and the name of the person addressed in the salutation of a letter and the first word in the closing of a letter—Dear Marie, Yours truly
- the first word, the last word, and each important word in the titles of books, plays, works of art, and poems—*Ramona the Brave, Starry Night,* "Keep a Poem in Your Pocket"
- the first word of a direct quotation—Mother said, "It's time for my favorite television program."
- proper adjectives—American flag, Dutch cocoa

Capital letters are also used for

- the pronoun *I*
- two-letter state postal abbreviations—MA, NY, CA
- an initial (a capital letter followed by a period). A person may use an initial instead of a name—C. S. Lewis.

COMPARISONS

Many adjectives can be used to compare two or more people, places, or things.

- To compare two people, places, or things, add *-er* to most adjectives: *taller, cuter, hungrier, bigger.*
- To compare three or more people, places, or things, add *-est* to most adjectives: *meanest, nicest, happiest, hottest.*
- If an adjective ends in *e (brave),* drop the final *e* and add *-er* or *-est: braver, bravest.*
- If an adjective ends in *y* following a consonant *(lucky)*, change the *y* to *i* and add *-er* or *-est*: *luckier, luckiest.*
- If a short adjective ends in a consonant that follows a vowel *(mad)*, double the final consonant before adding *-er* or *-est*: *madder, maddest.*
- Some adjectives that compare are **irregular adjectives**: *good, better, best* and *bad, worse, worst.*

CONJUNCTIONS

A **conjunction** is a word used to connect words or groups of words.

A **coordinating conjunction** connects words or groups of words that are similar. The most common coordinating conjunctions are the words *and, but,* and *or*: Joshua *or* Leanne will cut out the words. Nancy drew *and* colored the pictures. Mika glued the words on the poster, *but* Carla glued the pictures.

CONTRACTIONS

A **contraction** is two words written as one word with one or more letters missing. An apostrophe (') is used to show where a letter or letters have been taken out. The word *not* is often part of a contraction: *aren't = are not, don't = do not, won't = will not.*

NOUNS

A **noun** is a word that names a person, a place, or a thing.

A **common noun** names any one member of a group of people, places, or things: *queen, city, church.*

A **proper noun** names a particular person, place, or thing. A proper noun begins with a capital letter: *Queen Elizabeth, London, Westminster Abbey.*

A **singular noun** names one person, place, or thing: *boy, ranch, berry.*

A **plural noun** names more than one person, place, or thing.

- To form the plural of a **regular noun,** add *-s* or *-es*: *boys, ranches.*
- If a regular singular noun ends in a consonant followed by *y* (*berry, fairy*), change the *y* to *i* and add *-es*: *berries, fairies.*
- If a regular singular noun ends in a vowel followed by *y* (*monkey*), add *-s*: *monkeys.*
- The plural of an **irregular noun** is not formed by adding *-s* or *-es*: *men, children, wolves, teeth, fish.*

A **collective noun** names a group of people or things that are considered as a unit: The *band* played loudly.

A noun used in **direct address** names the person spoken to: *Carol,* would you help me?

A **possessive noun** expresses possession or ownership. The apostrophe (') is the sign of a possessive noun.

- To form the possessive of a singular noun, add *-'s* to the singular form: *architect's.*
- To form the possessive of a plural noun that ends in *-s*, add an apostrophe to the plural form: *farmers'.*
- To form the possessive of a plural noun that does not end in *-s*, add *-'s* to the plural form: *children's.*

PRONOUNS

A **pronoun** is a word that takes the place of a noun. A **personal pronoun** has different forms.

A **plural** pronoun refers to more than one person, place, or thing. The plural pronouns are *we, us, ours, you, yours, they, them,* and *theirs.*

A **singular** pronoun refers to one person, place, or thing. The singular pronouns are *I, me, mine, you, yours, she, her, hers, he, him, his, it,* and *its.*

A **subject pronoun** may be used as the subject of a sentence. The subject pronouns are *I, you* (singular or plural), *he, she, it, we,* and *they*: *He* bought a new car. *You* look great, Carrie!

- A compound subject may contain one or more subject pronouns. The subjects are connected by the word *and* or *or*: *He* and Margie are in the park. Joe and *she* are playing tennis. *He* or *she* will win the game.

An **object pronoun** may be used after the action verb in a sentence. The object pronouns are *me, you* (singular or plural), *him, her, it, us,* and *them*: I saw *her* at the mall. I saw *you* at the mall, Kevin.

A **possessive pronoun** shows possession or ownership. The possessive pronouns are *mine, yours, his, hers, its, ours,* and *theirs.* They never come before nouns. Although possessive pronouns show ownership, they do not contain apostrophes: The new skates are *hers.* That canoe is *ours.*

See also **Sentences, Subject-Verb Agreement.**

PUNCTUATION

Punctuation is used to make writing clearer.

An **apostrophe** (') is used as follows:

- to show ownership—the *cook's* hat, the *girls'* horses, the *children's* toys
- to replace letters left out in a contraction—*isn't* for *is not, don't* for *do not*

A **comma** (,) can be used in many ways, including the following:

- to separate words or groups of words in a series—We saw elephants, giraffes, hyenas, and monkeys.
- to set off parts of addresses—321 Spring Rd., Apt. 4
- to separate a city and a state—Atlanta, Georgia
- to set off parts of dates—June 12, 2010
- to set off words in direct address—Josie, I'm so pleased that you called me this morning.
- to set off a direct quotation—"We have only vanilla and chocolate today," he explained.
- to separate simple sentences connected by the conjunctions *and, but,* and *or*—She called his name, but he didn't answer her.
- after the salutation in a friendly letter and the closing in all letters—Dear Ben, Sincerely yours,

An **exclamation point** (!) is used at the end of an exclamation: What a celebration that was!

A **period** (.) is used in these ways:

- at the end of a telling sentence—His dog ran away.
- at the end of a command—Please find him.
- after many abbreviations—Dr. = Doctor, ft. = feet.

A **question mark** (?) is used at the end of a question: What time is it?

Quotation marks (" ") are used as follows:

- before and after every direct quotation—"Let's go shopping," said Michiko. Father said, "I haven't eaten lunch."
- to enclose titles of poems—"What I Left Where"

SENTENCES

A **sentence** is a group of words that expresses a complete thought. A sentence has a subject and a predicate.

The **subject** names who or what a sentence is about.

- The **simple subject** is a noun or a pronoun: The *man* is riding his bike.
- The **complete subject** is the simple subject and all the words that go with it: *The tall young man* is riding his bike.
- A subject pronoun may be used as the subject of a sentence: *We* went to the mall.
- If a sentence has more than one simple subject, it has a **compound subject**: *Ivan* and *John* argued with the grocer.

The **predicate** tells something about the subject.

- The **simple predicate** is a verb or a verb phrase: Teresa *waved.*
- The **complete predicate** is the verb and all the words that go with it: Teresa *waved from the window.*
- If a sentence has more than one simple predicate, it has a **compound predicate**: Our hamster *eats* and *exercises* at night.

A **subject complement** can follow a being verb. A subject complement is an adjective that describes the subject: The boy was *angry.*

A **compound sentence** contains two short sentences that are related to each other. They are combined with a comma, followed by the word *and, but,* or *or.* We went to the park, *and* we played softball. It started to rain, *but* we kept playing.

A **command** tells what to do. It is usually ends with a period: Go to the store. Please pick up the papers.

An **exclamation** expresses strong or sudden emotion. It ends with an exclamation point: What a loud noise that was!

A **question** is an asking sentence. It ends with a question mark and often starts with a question word: Where is my pen?

Handbook of Terms

A **run-on sentence** is a sentence in which two sentences are combined incorrectly: We will play checkers, we will watch a movie. To correct a run-on sentence, add the word *and, but,* or *or* after the comma. When a run-on sentence is corrected, it becomes a compound sentence: We will play checkers, *or* we will watch a movie.

A **statement** is a telling sentence. It ends with a period: The sun is shining.

SUBJECT-VERB AGREEMENT

A subject and its verb must agree.

- In the simple present tense, singular nouns and the singular pronouns *he, she,* and *it* take verbs that end in *-s* or *-es*: The boy *runs.* He *runs.*
- In the simple present tense, plural nouns, plural subject pronouns *(we, you, they)*, and the subject pronouns *I* and *you* take verbs that do not end in *-s* or *-es*: Horses *run.* We *run.* You *run.* They *run.* I *run.*
- Use *am* or *was* with the subject pronoun *I*: I *am* a soccer player. I *was* late for practice.
- Use *is* or *was* with a singular noun or with the subject pronouns *he, she,* and *it*: Paris *is* a city. She *was* a pianist.
- Use *are* or *were* with a plural noun or with the subject pronouns *you, we,* and *they*: Dogs *are* good pets. You *are* the winner. You *are* all winners. We *were* happy. They *were* my neighbors.

TENSES

The tense of a verb shows when its action happens.

- The **simple present tense** tells about something that is always true or about an action that happens again and again: The sun *rises* in the east. I *play* the piano every afternoon.
- The **simple past tense** tells about an action that happened in the past. The simple past of a regular verb is formed by adding *-d* or *-ed*: I *played* the piano yesterday afternoon. The simple past of an irregular verb is not formed by adding *-d* or *-ed*: I *sang*. They *wrote.* She *sat.*
- The **future tense** tells about an action that will happen in the future. The future tense can be formed in two ways. One way is to use the helping verb *will* and the present part of a verb: They *will visit* the museum on Sunday.

- Another way to form the future tense is to use *am going to, is going to,* or *are going to* with the present part of the verb: I *am going to play* shortstop.
- The **present progressive tense** tells what is happening now. The present progressive tense is formed with *am, is,* or *are* and the present participle: He *is eating* his lunch now.
- The **past progressive tense** tells what was happening in the past. The past progressive tense is formed with *was* or *were* and the present participle: He *was eating* his lunch when I saw him.

See also **Subject-Verb Agreement, Verbs.**

VERBS

An **action verb** is a word tells what someone or something does: Jake *sings.* The dog *barked.*

A **being verb** shows what someone or something is. Being verbs do not express action. Sometimes a being verb is used to join the subject of a sentence to an adjective: He *is* happy. The bag *was* heavy.

A **helping verb** is a verb that is always followed by a main verb. Some helping verbs are *am, is, are, was, were, be, being, been, shall, will, may, can, has, have, had, do, does, did, should, would, could,* and *must*: Mom *is washing* the dishes. I *will help* her.

A verb has four **principal parts**: the **present,** the **present participle,** the **past,** and the **past participle.**

- The present participle is formed by adding *-ing* to the present: *jumping, writing, hopping.* The present participle is used with a form of the helping verb *be*: I *am jumping.* She *was writing.* They *are hopping.*
- The past and the past participle of **regular verbs** are formed by adding *-d* or *-ed* to the present: *jump, jumped.* The past participle is used with a form of the helping verb *have*: I *have jumped.* She *has written.* They *had hopped.*
- The past and the past participle of **irregular verbs** are not formed by adding *-ed* to the present: *sang, sung.*

See also **Subject-Verb Agreement, Tense.**